Jamais Arriere

THE POEMS OF

STEWART DOUGLAS

Copyright 2014 by Christopher M. Moors

All rights reserved. No part of this book may be used or reproduced in any manner whatsoever without written permission, except in the case of brief quotations embodied in critical articles or reviews.

ISBN-10: 0985697962
ISBN-13: 978-0-9856979-6-9

Published 2014 by the Creative Cosmos

Printed in the United States of America

Foreward

Using my grandfather William S. Moors' compilation of the poems of Stewart Douglas as a guide, I've kept my interventions to a minimum. I also reviewed the originals of my great-great grandfather Stewart Douglas extensively and in detail. This provided me plenty of source material to publish an authentic version of the work.

It reveals a pioneer and community leader with a sense of moral responsibility.

This is truly a work that spans the generations.

Christopher M. Moors

Preface

Stewart S. Douglas was born on Eddlewood Row in Hamilton, Scotland on November 17, 1878 to John Douglas, an illiterate Coalpitheadsman and Sarah (Mooney) Douglas, who were married in 1855 in County Derry, Ireland.

Stewart Douglas married Helen Bradley, and had four children, John and Margaret who were born in Scotland, and Evelyn and Anne who were born in the United States. They settled in Bay City, Michigan, where Helen's brother, John Bradley and wife Evelyn also resided.

He was employed for many years in the engineering department at the Industrial Brownhoist Company of Bay City. That firm was engaged in making heavy cranes for the construction business. During that time, he was a deacon/lay minister for the First Baptist Church of Bay City, and for many years filled in as minister for the Essexville Baptist Church. Shortly before his retirement from the Industrial Brownhoist, he became an ordained minister, retiring in 1955. He died a few years later.

His poems range in date from about 1920 to 1950 and cover a number of topics.

Admittedly, at times he stretched "poetic license" in order to make a poem work, but in my opinion, that is secondary to the messages he was trying to convey.

His poems also provide a window to the inner man.

Within our family, he was regarded as the patriarch-----a reputation justly earned.

William S. Moors

Dedicated to those grandparents
Who often do not realize
The impact they are having
On their grandchildren

TABLE OF CONTENTS

ACME	1
ACROSS THE STREET	2
AFTER	3
AFTERMATH	4
AMERICA BOWS THE KNEE	5
AMERICA, EVER FOR ME	6
AMERICA ON THE BATTLEFIELDS OF FRANCE	7
ANCESTORS	8
AN OLD TIME SHEIK	9
ARE YOU A BROTHER OF MINE	10
AS WE APPEAR	11
A THANKSGIVING THOUGHT	12
AT THE BARBERS ON SATURDAY NIGHT	13
THE BADGE OF A SCOUT	15
BAY CITY	16
BAY CITY – KEEP PLUGGING	17
THE BEAUTIFUL SNOW	18
BE STILL	19
BEYOND TELLING	20
BIRTHDAY WISH FOR EFFIE	21
BLAMING GOD	22
THE BOSS SYSTEM	23
BUDDY BOY	24
THE CALL OF THE SEA	26
THE CALL OF THE WILD	27
CHALLENGE OF THE FLAG	28
COME NEAR	29
COMMON SIGHTS	30
COMRADESHIP	31
CONTRAST	32
COURAGE	33
CRIPPLED AMERICA	34
DAWN	36
A DAY IN CADILAC	37
THE DAY'S VISION	38
DO YOU RING TRUE?	39
A DRIPPING DAY	40

THE DYING DAY	41
ETERNAL	42
EXCHANGE	43
FAITH	44
FATHER	45
FATHER'S KNOW TOO MUCH	46
A FELLOW'S SISTER	47
FEVERED	48
THE FINEST SIGHT	49
FOR AYE	50
A FRIEND IN NEED	51
GETTING BY	53
GIVEN THE LAUGH	54
GOD	55
GOD EVERYWHERE	56
GOOD BOOKS	57
A GOOD INVESTMENT	58
HAD WE BUT KNOWN	59
THE HIGHER WAY	60
THE HIGHEST KINSHIP	61
HOPE SUCCEEDS HOPE	62
I SHALL NOT THINK OF DEATH	63
IF THE SUN ALWAYS SHONE	64
INTERDEPENDENTS	65
INTERROGATION	66
THE ISSUES OF LIFE	67
IT'S A GIFT	68
IT'S UP TO YOU	69
JUDGEMENT	70
JUST YOU AND ME TOGETHER	71
KEEP IN THE HARNESS	72
THE KINDLY DAY	73
KNOTS	74
THE LARGER GOD	75
LEAVES	76
LESSONS	77
LIGHT OF CHRISTMAS	78
LIKE SHIPS THAT SAIL	79

THE LURE AND THE BLESSING	80
MAKE IT SHORT	81
THE MASTER BUILDER PASSES ON	82
THE MASTER PIPER	83
THE MEANING OF CHRISTMAS	85
A MICHIGAN GIRL	86
A MICHIGAN MAN	87
MICHIGAN WOODS	88
A MIGHTY PRESENCE	89
THE MINER	91
THE MISERY OF SIN	92
THE MISTS ARE LIFTING	93
MONSTERS	94
THE MOTHER OF MY BOYS	95
MOTHER TO DAUGHTER	96
MOTHER'S DAY SONG	97
MUSIC	98
MUTUALITY	99
MY MICHIGAN HOME	100
MY OLD TATTERRRED BOOKS	101
MY WISH	102
THE NEEDS OF THE HOUR	103
THE NEW DAY	104
NO SUBSTITUTE	105
ODE TO KIPLING	106
ONLY A QUARTER	107
OPPORTUNITY	108
O WHAT A GOOD OLD WORLD	109
THE PARAMOUNT QUESTION	110
PARENT OR FATHER?	111
A PARTY FEELING	112
PASSING	113
PASS ON	114
PERPETUAL VACATION	115
A PRESENT FOR A WEDDING	116
THE PRISON	117
THE QUEST	118
THE REAL AMERICAN	119
REAL LOVE	120

THE REMEDY	121
RICHES	122
THE RIVER OF LIFE	123
THE ROAD TO BETHLEHEM	124
ROAD TO THE STARS	125
ROOSEVELT	126
ROYALTY	127
THE SAGINAW RIVER	128
SAME OLD	129
A SAVING REMEMBRANCE	130
SAY IT NOW	131
THE SCOURGE	132
SHALL WE CHANGE OUR PLAN	134
SHIFTING THE BLAME	135
THE SILVER SIX	136
SMILING MICHIGAN	137
SOURCES OF STRENGTH	138
THE SPARROW	139
STARS LOOK DOWN	140
STRIPES	141
A STROLL IN THE RAIN	142
THE SUCCESS OF SUCCESS	143
A THANKSGIVING HOPE	144
THAT'S A DIFFERENT STORY	145
THE TASK OF A MAN	146
THEIR STANDARD	147
THERE'S SOMETHING TO BE DONE	148
THOUGHTS IN A CHURCHYARD	149
THOUGHTS IN THE OPEN	150
THOUGHTS ON EASTER	151
TOAST OF THE FATHERS TO THE SONS	152
TO A YOUNG MOTHER	153
TOGETHER	154
THE TRAIL OF THE KING	155
TRANSCENDENT AMERICA	156
TRUE DESIRE	157
TRYING SITUATIONS	158
TWO ROSES	159

UNPAID	160
THE VANITY OF WORDS	161
VALUES	162
WELCOME	163
WHAT A SMILE MAY DO	164
WHAT MORTALS WE	165
WHAT OF YOU	166
WHEN MA'S AWAY	167
WOMAN	168
THE WONDERFUL JEW	169
WONDERS	172
THE WORST KIND	173
A YOUNG LAUGH	174

ACME

If our dishes and meals were near our ideals,
If our wishes brought all to our door,
If no man was caught with a snag in his thought,
What a soundness we'd have at the core.
If each of us had just a millionaire dad,
And his money was free as the snow,
Then river and plain could be cross'd without strain,
And we'd glide without having to row.

If we just had our way we'd always be gay,
We would laugh all our cares to the wind,
We'd travel along to the tune of a song,
And the whole world would be of one mind.
But the ACME of gain is sunshine and rain,-
The thought makes our heart burn within,-
Could hair black or red but return to our head,
Could we only grow bald on the chin!

Stewart Douglas
July 2, 1931

ACROSS THE STREET

Across the street the chimes were pealing
Music on the still night air,
From out of the church soft strains came stealing,
Washing from the night its care.
Across the street! It seemed my mentor,
Forced my then unwilling feet, -
The doors swung back for me to enter,
Where I humbly took my seat.

The message, it was throbbing, thrilling,
Chinese missions was the text,
Ardor every heart seemed filling,
Yet it left me strangely vexed.
Money poured, great offerings given, -
Just to give, some fain would sell -
The Chinese must be given Heaven,-
Just across the street, 'twas hell.

Across the street again I'm wending
Back beside the pain and woe,
Where living problems seem unending,-
Back where evolution's slow.
Back where thoughts of missions foreign
Seem to be so out of place,
Back where homes and hearts and hopes forlorn
Lie outside the pale of grace.

Our missions, God defend them ever,
Keep them growing fast and sure,
But first across the street or never
Lies our task, the Christian's lure, -
Evoke the smile of Heav'n o'ertopping,
On the heathen - this is meet -
But now the tears of God are dropping
For the folks across the street.

Stewart Douglas

AFTER

Last night was more than three weeks long,
But what a golden dawn, -
And I will sing my loudest, for,
Tomorrow I'll be gone.

Last night was lonesome, void of song,
Today my friends appear, -
And I will be so friendly, for, -
Tomorrow's never here.

Last night was blind and full of doubt,
Today I'm round the bend, -
The path I'll light so brightly, for, -
Tomorrow worlds may end.

Stewart Douglas

AFTERMATH

Enthuse, when the war drums are beating,
Enthuse, when vast armies are meeting,
Advancing, entrenching, retreating,
And Hell's thunder rolls o'er the deep.
Enthuse when the cannons are roaring,
Enthuse for the death they are pouring,
Enthuse for the Vict'ry you're scoring,
But tomorrow, -- tomorrow you'll weep.

Prepare for the next coming battle,
For the slaughter of men and of cattle -
O foolish, nonsensical prattle!
For death is wrapped up in that way.
Draw the sword in the wrongs you are righting,
Train your forces and soon you'll be fighting,
And war must ensue, stark and blighting,
But tomorrow, tomorrow you'll pay.

Enthuse, when vast armies are drilling,
Enthuse, 'tis a great sight and thrilling,
Enthuse, you'll be in at the killing,
To gratify men in their greed.
Keep building your battle-ships bigger,
Increasing your annual "figger",
Keep your finger each day on the trigger,
And tomorrow, tomorrow you'll bleed.

What a heritage on we are passing,
What woes for the unborn amassing,
What hearts we are crushing, harassing,
By war's ugly specter of dread.
Keep your armament factories running,
The peace of humanity shunning,
And for others you're bound to go "gunning",
But tomorrow, you'll bury your dead.

Stewart Douglas

AMERICA BOWS THE KNEE

Unequaled grace, unnumbered gifts, have touched our lives again.
Thanksgiving's here, with smiling cheer, God's goodness in its train.
And whether scars or whether wounds or whether joys or tears,
Have changed the night, or dimmed the light, or cast aside our fears,
For what we are, cemented strong, and true from shore to shore,
A nation great, with hearts elate, and loyal to the core, -
A nation strong with arteries fed, O Lord of hosts by Thee,
For all of this our country's bliss, America bows the knee.

Unfettered land! Where freedom's robe is worn by one and all,
A land of health and shining wealth, where men may rise who fall;
A land of hope and smiling hearts, where joy to youth is given,
Compared with lands on other strands, America lives in Heaven.
So whether in the desert sand or in the valley green,
In arctic cold, or summer fold, in waking hours or dream,
With reverent hearts today we turn amid our children's glee,
For every gift and every lift, America's Thanking Thee.

Stewart Douglas

AMERICA, EVER FOR ME

We sat by the campfire one evening,-
We thought of the lands o'er the sea.
Of the wealth and the health of old England,
and the glory of gay old Paree.
Of beauteous spots where the sunlight streamed
over the hills to the sea,
But no land howe'er fair can with this one can compare,
America, ever for me.

I want to stay here in the homeland,
I want to stay here with the free.
I want to stay here in the homeland,
Tho all the world beckons to me.
I want to stay here where the shadows,
By the light of her emblem shall flee,
I want to stay here in the homeland,
America, ever for me.

We thought of the green hills of Erin,
and the hearts ever there rich and true,
Of the grandeur and glory of Scotia,
and the land of the wild caribou.
Of lands where the rich, golden sunset
with glory filled meadow and lea,
But the home of the brave,
my heart ever will crave,
America, ever for me.

Stewart Douglas

AMERICA ON THE BATTLEFIELDS OF FRANCE

The world was wrapped in gloom, it seemed the knell of doom,
Had sent its baleful note across the Earth.
When o'er the weeping world the flag of hope unfurled.
Raised hearts from sorrow's depths to joy and mirth,
Across the leaden sky, writ large the battle cry.
For freedom's rights America, advance,
But now in song and story read America's full glory,
Her glory on the battlefields of France.

Her glory ne'er shall die – long live the battle cry,
America, for freedom's rights, advance.
The whole world knows the story of America, full glory,
Her glory on the battlefields of France.

The night of terror past, the day has dawned at last,
When men the wide world o'er may clasp the hand.
America the brave – her blood she freely gave,
The blood of all the best born in the land.
As long as time shall roll men will ne'er forget the toll,
That cut our nation's heart with sorrow's lance.
The valor shown in Flanders will for ever speak the wonders,
Of our glory in the battlefields of France.

Stewart Douglas

ANCESTORS

I used to trace my forbears down a long and ancient line,
Down to all the old aristocrats along the smiling Rhine,
Down to gentlemen from England, from Virginia and from Main,
While my Mother's great grandfather was a courtly Don is Spain.
But their glory all has faded, I'm not feeling quite so proud,
My ancestors had ancestors, whom I will not name so loud.
And I'm mortified to think it, it's like standing in a bog,
For they say that I'm related to a wiggling pollywog.

I used to read my hist'ry, now for that I've lost all taste,
I can't think quite so clearly, since my pedigree's disgraced.
The tears start slowly sometimes, then I laugh and prance and shout,
And I'm damning all the Darwins, till the Darwins start a rout,
And an able lecture downs me, then again I'm filled with glee,
For the other side is winning, then once more I put to sea,
Where the howling wastes assail me, and I'm back where I began,
Where the horse becomes a donkey, and a monkey makes a man.

But at last I'm growing calmer, on my problems I have smiled,
My instructors, and opponents, they may yet be reconciled,
For there's work to do a plenty, if we'd bring our stock to par -
We must do a little something for the monkeys now that are;
We must cultivate their manners, we must teach them wisdom too,
So that later, not a monkey will be found within a Zoo,-
So that later like their hybrids, like the men they have produced,
They'll be proud of their ancestors, when they're being introduced.

Stewart Douglas
Read at First Baptist Church, Bay City, 16 December 1932

AN OLD TIME SHEIK

If colors speak a language
That's sincere and never lies,
Will someone please interpret
What's behind a woman's eyes.

There's Anne whom I have fondly loved,
Her eyes of hazel brown
Have whispered many a secret joy,
Since she has come to town.

There's Margaret loved a whit not less,
Whose eyes of liquid blue
Have often made a fool of me, -
Perhaps a fool of you.

There's Effie who now keeps my heart,
You'll read it in her eyes,
But that's just three and let me say,
That each of them's a prize.

There's Helen whom I've loved so long,
She's number four but first,
Her glowing eyes have often quenched
My soul's deep raging thirst.

So now confessed—your thoughts run wild, -
A riot in your brain,
You'd turn me out without a brief,
And leave me in the rain.

But wait before your words unleashed,
Fall cuttingly on me, -
Four women I'm entitled to,
One wife, and daughters three.

Stewart Douglas
Read at a party in Essexville

ARE YOU A BROTHER OF MINE

He's distinguished by lands and possessions,
And to these e'er so many bow down,
Or else he has gained his distinction,
From his family name of renown.
But whether from deeds full of merit,
Be he monied or not worth a dime,
If the heart of a gentleman's in him
I know he's a brother of mine.

He's distinguished perhaps by his learning -
Erudition's the road oft to fame
Tho sometimes the famed have been tempted,
To ask what there is in a name.
Mayhap he's the world's finest artist,
And in music has reached the divine,
Yet what is his heart, that's a man's biggest part,
If it's right, he's a brother of mine.

He's distinguished by hands that are roughened,
You can tell he's at true son of toil,
He can't hide the fact nor would if he could,
This builder, this tiller of soil.
But it's not how a man earns his living,
The right to drink water or wine,
But what he has done for his fellows
That makes him a brother of mine.

So whether distinguished by money,
By heart, deeds, or letters, or fame,
Or whether you toil in the broil of the day
Or live off the spoils of the game.
If the need of your fellows you're spurning -
You could rescue, but won't throw the line,
Not a part of the gentleman's in you,
And you ne'er were a brother of mine.

Stewart Douglas

AS WE APPEAR

The stars look down from their vaulted heights
On the fitful scenes below,
On the usual sights of the lighted nights
Where men pass to and fro,
Where the tearless eye and the haughty mien
Wots not of the woe or pain
That others glean tho' their souls are clean
After sewing the golden grain.

The stars look down; do they look in vain?
Or are they but soulless orbs?
Could their knowledge pass to these hearts of brass
There might be responsive chords,
And the undimmed eye and the barren pride
Of the slumbering sons of men,
Like mists of the night would vanish from sight
And would never return again.

But the stars look down and continue to stare,
As they've stared for weary years
On the pain and joy of the man and boy,
And the stars have shed their tears.
And the selfish years of the world roll on
And countless lives are shriven,
By harshness of men, the world's greatest bane
And the greatest surprise to Heaven.

Stewart Douglas

A THANKSGIVING THOUGHT

For gleaming lights that lead us,
For kindly hearts that need us,
For mountains we have climbed,
For hills made low,
For Red Seas that have parted,
For loved ones warm hearted,
For mercies that have never ceased to flow,
For Dawning's baffling glory,
For Evening's soothing story,
For wordless thought that strengthens and defends
For these our hearts are saying,
"Thanks a Million", Lord, and praying,
A generous double portion for our friends.

Stewart Douglas

AT THE BARBERS ON SATURDAY NIGHT

I had put it off for a number of weeks,
Or maybe a month or two,
'Till I looked like one of the many freaks
That pass you in daily review.
But it had to be cut, - you've been in the same fix -
And I surely was looking a fright,
So I started to stroll at a quarter of six,
To the barber's on Saturday night.

When I entered, the barber was pasting the Mayor
And tearing the Council to shreds,
His helper, who looked like a modern slayer,
Was defending with vigor the reds.
An old man who looked like the days of the flood,
Was doing the preachers up brown:
You would almost believe, - for he could "throw the mud"-
That the preachers had ruined the town.

"'Tis a terrible state," said another, whose head
Was as bald as the back of my hand,
"That a man has to labor so hard for his bread,
While the wealthy own all of the land."
Then the head of our State came in for his share -
His morals were not worth a cent.
And our Senate and Congress were wrapped in despair
Because of the President's bent.

My neighbor I thought I had known till that night,
Tho I'd lived twenty years by his side,
To me Bill had always lived plainly and right -
But this gossip said simply he lied.
But my faith in mankind was too strong for such stuff,
I had known my old neighbor too long -
These swaggering tongues were but throwing a bluff,
In their hearts sure they knew they were wrong.

My hair at last cut at a quarter to ten,
I started for home there and then.
But my thoughts would recur to the language I heard
In that polished tonsorial den.
Then I thought of the way I've heard some females talk -
Just as natural as fishes a-swimmin'.
But it's science with us - and we win in a walk,
Tho we've long passed the buck to the women.

Stewart Douglas
December 7, 1923

THE BADGE OF A SCOUT

They're with us to stay with their vigor and pep,
The boys who have gained such a national "rep" -
The boys who are building for future and weal -
The boys who will grow into men who are real.
Youthful and hopeful and brave boys and true,
Life will be handing her prizes to you.
For Life picks the winner in all of her bouts,
And places big odds on the boys who are Scouts.

And when we are with you and watching your play
Our own hearts are lighter, our own spirits gay,
For well do we know while we're watching you thus
You're laying the basis for energy plus,
You're building in loyalty, courage and truth -
Building it into the years of your youth -
Building true manhood beyond faithless doubts
By the strength and the program of red-blooded Scouts.

So boys, you are splendid in all that you do,
The heart of Old Glory's depending on you.
But a Scout never fails; 'tis part of his creed,
He'll answer each call when there's plainly a need -
He'll stand by his colors, forsake not his post,
A Scout will be faithful whatever the cost.
He'll rally and help with a courage that's stout,
For Honor and Virtue's the badge of a Scout.

Stewart Douglas

BAY CITY

I came to your city enroute to the north,
I stopped for a day to study its worth.
Its loveliness 'thralled me, I felt its repose,
I lingered, for this was the city I chose.
A city I found to be cleaner than most,
Whether laden with flowers or sprinkled with frost,
Then here's to its heart, to its life and its spirit,
Its strength and its singular beauty and merit.

Singular merit? Yes gaze while the breeze,
Hums a glad song thru its wonderful trees.
Cast your eyes east ere the day's work be done,
Where the lake crystallizes so clear in the sun.
Look with unprejudiced eyes from the west,
To the white, rippling lights on Water Street's breast,
Look! And with haste you will form a committee,
To speak forth the praise of your wonderful city.

Wonderful city? Yes, look at its site,
To forty three millions and outlet of might,
Beckoning outward, her claims yet denied,
She stands on the Saginaw strong in her pride.
Strong in her pride, a city serene,
With garments of beauty, 'mong cities a queen.
Quietful and peaceful - 'tis only a pity,
I stayed quite so long from your charming Bay City.

Stewart Douglas
June 10, 1931

BAY CITY – KEEP PLUGGING

Comely, O Queen of the valley, and happy
Gracing the mouth of old Saginaw Bay
Cleanly and healthful, virile and snappy
Hail to the city so verdant and gay
Clad in the beauty of nature's own weaving
Known for its elegant site far and wide
Strong in big faith and with energy cleaving -
Your hope of the future shall not be denied.

Press on then O Queen of the Saginaw Valley
Your thousands are fifty, they ought to be more
And will when the forces within you shall rally -
And rise to the standard that opens the door.
Our faith's in the future when every lone faction
Shall group all its energies into a whole
But now old Bay City's the time for strong action
Keep plugging, keep boosting, keep saving your soul.

Stewart Douglas

THE BEAUTIFUL SNOW

Over the world a garment of white,
O Beautiful, Beautiful snow,
Gleamingly cold and a dazzling sight
O Beautiful, Beautiful snow.
Highways are buried and pathways lost,
Passengers huddled, jostled and tossed,
Ditches are straddled but never crossed
O Beautiful, Beautiful snow.

White as the soul of a little child,
O Beautiful, Beautiful snow.
Falling so gently you've driv'n me wild
O Beautiful Beautiful snow.
Somewhere the poets are chanting your praise,
Somewhere motors are groaning sweet lays, -
My car's been stalled for several days,
O Beautiful, Beautiful snow.

Three feet of snow - encouraging pile,
O Beautiful, Beautiful snow,
After the storm you tell me to smile,
O Beautiful, Beautiful snow.
My back is bent, my shovel is full
Beautiful snow I'm only your tool,
So Heaven help this shoveling fool,
O Beautiful, Beautiful snow.

Hedges of snow along ev'ry line,
O Beautiful, Beautiful snow.
Hiding the grass where the sparrows dine,
O Beautiful, Beautiful snow.
Looking like mud, grimy and sooty,
We love your crystal, wintry, beauty,
As all men love a painful duty,
O Beautiful, Beautiful snow.

Stewart Douglas

BE STILL

Hold thy peace, it will be thy wisdom,
    The presence of Jehovah's near;
The stilly hour is God's own choosing,
    The still small voice will silence fear.

Stewart Douglas

BEYOND TELLING

We speak of her love and we know it is great -
Far beyond any love that we know,
A love like the rivers that run to the sea
With their constant and unchanging flow.
And we'll herald that love and we'll praise her on Earth
Till the last of her victories is won;
But we must not forget Mother's other fine works
And the things for the race she has done.

We speak of her faith and it fills us with awe
As we look in her wonderful eyes,
Tho her child takes the path that as crooked and rough
The light of her faith never dies.
In this she's alone, for no mortal may reach
Such a height on this side of the sun.
But our Mothers, - God bless them! We must not forget
The other great things they have done.

We'll speak of her love, of her faith and her worth -
Of her patience, her courage, her cheer -
Of her tenderness, beauty, the grace of her form -
And we'll love her as long as we're here.
We may gather together a world of great deeds,
We may single them out one by one -
But no one will ever be able to tell
Just all that our Mothers have done.

Stewart Douglas
October 29, 1923

BIRTHDAY WISH FOR EFFIE

What shall I wish for you today
Since one more year has come your way? -
A woman's charm but not her wiles?
One lone frown per thousand smiles?
Ambitions not too high, nor low?
A liberal heart for friend and foe?
From every woman's faults set free,
Retaining still her mystery?
If these were all that came from dad, -
Well, Effie dear, you'd think me mad.

So let me very simply say,
The very best for you today!
May deeper love come "out your way",
And truer friends be there to stay.

Stewart Douglas
January 20, 1940

Effie was 'Evelyn', daughter of Stewart and mother of William S. Moors.

BLAMING GOD

For everything on land or sea wisdom finds a cause,
Except when fierce depression prowls the Earth
We scan with scanty merit both our plain and mystic laws,
To find the meaning of the fireless hearth.
But after all our jargon like a rush of wind at night,
Like pictures of a pathway never trod,
We shift the heavy burden and we think we've found the Light
By charging the depression up to God.

For crime and greed and fully we can find a reason true,
We measure suns and planets in their course,
We know why verdant nature's green and why the sky is blue.
We calculate the pow'r of any force,
But economic blunders that consume the souls of men
And bows the world beneath an awful load,
Have far too many answers so with one accord and pen,
We charge the cruel matter up to God.

Charge nature's twist to mother, Ah! But not to motherhood.
Or trace it back a hundred years or more.
Charge poverty to brethren, Ah! But not to brotherhood,
The words a mere misnomer on our shore.
For wheat is fed to cattle while our bread lines we enlarge,
The jobless tread the long and thorny road, ----
It's distinctively ungodly for anyone to charge
The guilt of all humanity to God.

Stewart Douglas
During the Great Depression

THE BOSS SYSTEM

There's a day or an hour in the life of us all
For which we are hoping deep down in our soul,
It comes with its buoyant and clarion call,
It's the peak of ambition, the top of our goal.
But it's always a step further on in the race,
And there's always another stiff hurdle to cross,
But still undaunted we keep up the pace
For the lure of the hour when we'll be our own boss.

What phantoms we chase from the hour of our birth,
How sordid our thoughts of life's profit and loss,
How hopeless the quest for the things that have worth,
If bound to the day when we'll be our own boss.
For the close of the day will yet find it afar,
Though the dawn of the day found it near to our reach,
And this we will find wheresoever we are,
So list to the message I'm seeking to teach.

We've a boss in the cradle, a boss in the school,
We've a boss when we're learning our trade,
There is no exception to this binding rule,
The system was born, never made.
Our conscience, our country, our teacher, our wives,
The weather, the sky, and the turn of the sod,
These are the masters of all of our lives,
And over them all there is - - GOD.

Stewart Douglas

BUDDY BOY

Hello there little Buddy!
It's your papa now who speaks, -
I can hear the gentle rivers
I can see the swollen creeks -
And the little spades of childhood
Where we built the sandy peaks.

I can hear the sighing night winds
As they told their eerie tale,
I can see the dewy islets
That gave shelter to the quail.
I can feel the hours so endless,
The years, - or were they ticks
That lay between my summers five -
I wanted to be S I X.
I can hear the yelling injuns
As we played at Buff'lo Bill
From the twighlight 'till the moonlight
At the foot of Kelton's Hill.
I can see the burley "Bobby,"
I can almost hear him talk,
I can hear his laboured breathing
As he chased us round the block.

I can hear a million voices,
I can see a million smiles,
I can tread the road to childhood
Tho it's nigh a million miles.
I can see the shining glory
Of the only age that's free,
I can hear the happy laughter
Rippling back across the sea.
I can see those days of magic
I can live those hours of glee,
When I'm talking to you, Buddy,
When you're standing at my knee.
When I'm writing foolish verses

When - but hark! The birds are here.
And they're bringing me a message
And it's full of lively cheer.
They are telling me you're better,
That they missed you for a spell
And they're feeling very happy
Because Buddy's getting well,
And they're singing on the railing
Doing all their old time tricks,
And this is what they're singing,
"Buddy boy will soon be S I X!"

Stewart Douglas
1932

THE CALL OF THE SEA

Incomprehensible, unresting sea,
Above finite concept as tow'r the stars,
Majestic and weird, yet beckoning me
To watchers of peace or thunderous wars -
And follow I must where ever you lead,
Whate'er your temper, tumultuous, calm -
The tang of your breezes speaks of my need,
Your solitude teaches the measure of man.

And, uninterpreted, oft where I've stood
With only a plank betwixt me and death,
I'd drink the dregs of her ugliest mood
That left me only the gasp of a breath.
And always I'd ponder this mystery
'Twas closer to God on the tumbling sea.

Stewart Douglas

THE CALL OF THE WILD

The call of the mountain, the woodland, the river,
The loud swelling roar of the sea in my ear,
With voices insistent, alluring as ever
Come stealing my peace but leaving their cheer,
The cataract wild with its turbulent symbol
The wild sweeping rush of the wind o'er the moor
These are the test of the young and the nimble
I'm hearing the call of the wild with its lure.

My temples are throbbing, my heart is a pounding
The desolate places have even a call
Out where the ripples of joy are abounding
The desert, the valley, the solitude's thrall.
I'm kindred to all of the vastness of nature
I care for it least when it's gentle and mild
The seeing myself as a pigmy in stature
My blood courses fast at the call of the wild.

Stewart Douglas

CHALLENGE OF THE FLAG

See! There before the eyes of all the world it flutters free
Symbol of the hearts that wove its famous colors three,
Wove them in the glory and the perils of the past,
And spun the fabric from their lives that evermore shall last.

Unrestricted, unrestrained, the red, the white, the blue,
Blending with the morning and the evening's sunset hue,
Waving in its glory, thrilling age, inspiring youth,
Challenging our manhood by its purity and truth.

Emblem of a loyalty that's known around the world,
Where righteousness foregathers, this flag shall be unfurled
To smile with unfeigned friendship on the nations far and near, -
Unsullied flag of freedom! We salute you with a cheer.

Stewart Douglas

COME NEAR

I loved you so dear, forgive me the tear,
In your happiness now so complete
I can't hold it back with my soul on the rack
Though your life be with joy now replete.
You were with me but moments compared to the time
That may now separate us, my dear.
Yet in life and in death my whole being is thine,
Dear heart in my sorrow, come near.

Down the long, lonely trail, you must bear with me dear,
When you image so full in my heart
Brings a stab and a pain and a shadow of fear
For the years we may still be apart.
Oh! Why did you so twine your soul 'round my soul?
Yet these love-bonds I cherish – revere,
To meet you again will be life's highest goal,
Dear heart in the lone hours, come near.

My duty they say is to bury my woe
In the grave where your dear form now lies,
But ah! They who say it can ne'er fully know
How strong between us were the ties.
So heart of my heart do help me to bear
The shadow, the silence, the fear,
Come close, for I know you'll eternally care,
Dear heart through the long years, come near.

Stewart Douglas

COMMON SIGHTS

There are things in our lives that are common to all,
There are sights that are common and plenty,
Like those of an amateur chasing a ball,
Or the look of a pocket book empty.
But yet it's the sights that are highly supreme,
And they're common enough to our being,
Tho' many will think they are merely a dream-
Well, these are the sights I am seeing.

The clouds may be there with a heavy-set frown,
But the smiles are just lurking behind them,
And these are the end of the clouds and their crown,
Just beyond if you look you will find them.
There is doubt, there is dread, there is pain on the Earth,
To this all our lives are agreeing,
But yet there are things of a far nobler worth,
And these are the things I am seeing.

It needs not a seer or a prophet of life
To pierce thru the thought of the ages,
The things men have done in the calm and the strife
Can be done both by you and the sages,
Of course there's misfortune, and you're now below level,
Your silken tongued friends may be fleeing,
But yet I have faith that you'll baffle the Devil, -
Your triumph's the thing I am seeing.

And so there's a smile lurking back of each cloud,
There are joys for the pains that beset you,
Put on your best garment and cast off your shroud,
To the winds with the worries that fret you,
Your works may be bad, but I'm betting on you, -
It was God who first handed you being,
With such a fine start you must win don't you see, -
Are you seeing the things that I'm seeing?

Stewart Douglas

COMRADESHIP

Come, take a hold of my hand, old friend,
Come, take a hold of my hand.
For what care I what the world may say,
Just give me your hand in the old time way
Here in the light of the rising day.
Come, - just take a hold of my hand.

Come, take a hold of my hand, old chum,
Come, take a hold of my hand.
The world may have crowded you out, I know,
Like fish on the crest of an overflow,
But deep in my heart lives the old time glow.
So, - just take a hold of my hand.

Just take a hold of my hand, old friend,
Just take a hold of my hand.
The way has been rough and you're battle-scarred,
Just lean on me now, and lean on me hard -
We'll make it together, together, old pard.
So, - just take a hold of my hand.

Stewart Douglas

CONTRAST

Never a kind word spoken
Riven hearts and broken
Always a shadow o'er the sun
In the path of life that we have run
Always the chill of bleak December
Only the dying e'er remember
The evil that they have done

Often a deed of kindness
Lighting the hours of blindness
Chasing the shadows from the sun
In the path of life that we must run
Building a fire for Chill December
Only the living e'er remember
The good that they may have done.

Stewart Douglas

COURAGE

This is the kind that martyrs showed,
This is the kind that needs no goad,
This is the kind for any road,
If you would be a winner;
To stand for right though foes surround,
To stand though death your soul should pound,
To stand though Hell should gather round, -
Befriending saint and sinner.

This is the kind that bears the yoke,
Whose body bends beneath the stroke
To save a lesser soul from shock
Perchance a lonely neighbor;
That glories in the rendered deed,
That takes from out its own soul's need
The best another soul to feed
And thinks not of the labor.

This is the courage of the true,
This is the courage of the few,
This is the courage meant for you,
For you and not another;
To look beneath the outer rim,
To see the man and not his sin,
to clasp his hand - - encourage him -
For God made you his brother.

Stewart Douglas

CRIPPLED AMERICA

Past, present and future being lost in the struggle;
The gallant strength of a nation dwindling to the dust;
Her rich blood turning to water in view of the world;
Her proud beauteous plumage ruffled and bedraggled, -
Sinking beneath the weight of her often broken laws,
And thinking – "She's as good a man as she ever was."

Thinking she's in need of nothing because she is rich,
While thugs laugh in her face and tell her to go to Hell.
Dens on Main Street like warts on the face of a woman,
While the minions of her laws laughingly pass on,
Some holding grasping hands behind their backs, palms skyward,
Till the righteous become a hissing and a by-word.

Even the decent laugh and seem to take it as a joke.
But God knows it is no joke when white turns to scarlet,
When the strong man and the great drags himself thru the mud,
When the lad no longer looks to dad for protection, -
When the day grows dim and when the night begins to reel,
And when the devil leers drunken at the steering wheel.

A joke? Gray, grizzly, tragic, Plutonic boomerang,
Striking back to leave us half blind and wholly crippled,
And filling our mouths with excuses and searching for more.
Calling God to witness that the foreigner's to blame –
That America's not to blame – the blame's on our schools,
The blame is on our churches, the blame is on our fools.

God and the preacher and the teacher, - these are to blame.
High or low, the house, but not the inmates, is at fault.
Prohibition is the cause. God wot! "Thou shalt not kill,"
"Thou shalt not steal," – these create all murder and all theft
And thus we wail and rail against all our common laws
Till hope dies and faith weakens in any kind of cause.

And so before the world we stand crippled and helpless,
Unable to cope with the crimes within our borders,
Staggering and stunned by the bludgeoning of outlaws,
Money to squander but not enough to keep the peace, -
And so we go a-limping, like the halt and the lame, -
Cripplers of America, your sons will bear the shame.

Stewart Douglas

DAWN

From her bath of opalescence she come softly o'er the hills
And dons her wondrous princely gown of pearl
But like coquettes of the ballroom she changes as she wills
To snare the heart of peasant, king or earl.
Her fancy turns from pearl to green, to amber, pink and blue,
And gold and rose come tripping in her train,
Of all the arts are calling loud to see me as well as you
When morning breaks and God's revealed again.

She blushes, frowns, and hesitates, just like a girl in love,
She cast abroad her jewels on the leaves
The drab cold stones with crystals shine - our hearts are raised above
For he who sees the dawn in God believes.
The clouds she ruffles on the face of sleeping waters, calm
Thru forests deep her glory sweeps and reigns,
Her perfumed breath she carries to the heart and soul of man
'Till Heaven's own wine runs riot in his veins.

Of all the changes nature works in atmosphere or air
There's none so grand nor yet sublime as dawn.
Whether viewed from frozen northlands or from sunny lands and fair.
Or simply seen when breaking o'er your lawn.
Where'er I comes the hand of God with most exquisite skill
In art sublime portrays the soul of Heav'n.
The man who rises early for the morning's glory thrill
To him the blessings of the day are giv'n.

Stewart Douglas

A DAY IN CADILAC

I'm stopping in old Cadilac, enroute for Mackinaw,
Old Cadilac that borders on the twins.
I could not help my stopping for the service that I saw,
Was the smiling kind that touches you and wins.
Old Cadilac, how splendid is the sound of that old name,
How charming are the things for which it stands!
Its restful spots and shaded depths have earned the right to fame,
And its climate makes you use your brain and hands.

Old Cadilac, with reigning lakes and miles of beauteous sights,
Attractive beaches, splendid girls, and games,
With camping, dancing, music and the joy of lighted nights,
And the mother'ng smile of happy hearted dames.
I'm glad I saw your service, and I'm glad I stopped a day,
You're a hustling, busy place without a frown.
You've beauty, charm, and manners more than I could ever say,
And I've had my wrinkles straightened in your town.

Stewart Douglas

THE DAY'S VISION

Fair as the face of the sleeping world
In the first rose flush of the dawn
Your eyes like the beautiful shades of light
Stealing into your room o'er the lawn,
Your youth like the clear sparkling fountains
Of vigor, of joy, health and grace –
This is the vision that comes each day
That time and its cares can't efface.

Serener your face with its mother light
Than the calm of an Autumn sky,
I see the September glories shine
In the depths of your mother eye,
And blended lights that I can't describe
Play over your mother face -
This is the vision that comes each day
As the steps of Time I retrace.

But fair and serene as the past may be,
Tho' it lives with me every day,
The flush of the dawn and the Autumn calm
Are combined in the twilight's ray.
Tho' far down the sky glows the swift setting sun
Contented I'll be with life's race
If on to the end I may gaze with repose,
On the undying light of your face.

Stewart Douglas

DO YOU RING TRUE?

It's not what you're telling the boys alone,
Though all that you're telling is true,
It is not the preachments you give them at home
Alone that will make them true blue.
It's the heart of the man who is speaking,
It's the soul back of each simple deed,
That will bring the best joys in winning the boys
And teach them the truth of your creed.

It's not what you're giving the boys at all
But the thing that's behind your gift,
This is what counts with the big and the small -
This gives the boys a true lift.
So turn your eyes in if a leader you'd be,
Find out if you're only a "noise",
If there's anything there that's not on the square,
Cut it out for the sake of the boys.

Stewart Douglas

A DRIPPING DAY

Barren and desolate, bleak and bare,
Like the winter gray of a craggy shore,
Comes this dripping day, bringing its care,
Drenching with dreariness e'en to the core.

Doleful, monotonous, dull and drab,
Laden with misery, dark thoughted lore,
Beating and dripping while mem'ries stab
And skeletons stand just outside my door.

Gloomy and morbid, sordid, defac'd
A world pouring chagrin, pouring regret,
For sunlight squander'd, seasons of waste -
Tomorrow we'll live, your lesson forget.

Stewart Douglas
March 13, 1928

THE DYING DAY

The dying day, the dying day,
But look ye how it dies,
The crimson west in evening dress
Where God has draped the skies,
The soft-hued haze, the quiet expanse,
The twilight on the bay,
The gentle stir among the leaves –
This is the dying day.

The liquid notes, the mellowed hour,
A finite mind to grasp,
That peace, that beauty such as this
The arms of death may clasp.
Pass on ye day, if yours be death
Your ending is sublime,
And decked in wedding splendors
All eternity is thine.

Stewart Douglas

ETERNAL

They said that death would part us, you and me,
And place between our love the crystal sea;
That nevermore our love would flow or run
But only ebb beneath a heartless sun, -
They could not know the love of you and me
Was just a symbol of eternity.

How could they think that ought would ever rise
To hide from me your shining, seeking eyes,
When ev'ry eve unhinder'd I behold
A depth of love that time can not unfold -
That rises far above the azure skies
To conquer death – A love that never dies.

Stewart Douglas

EXCHANGE

Give me a day on the grassy slopes,
With the wind blowing thru my hair,
Away from the bonds of city life,
From the eyes that glower and glare,
Out from between its prison walls
Out where there's never a care,
Out with my soul in the cleansing wind,
And you'll give me a joy that's rare.

Give me a day at the foot of the crags,
Where the spray of the sea is felt,
Or give me a day on the lone wild moor,
Or out on the wind-swept veldt,
Or out where the silence is golden
And the ether is crystal and clear,
Or give me a day by a murmuring brook
And I'll give you my city year.

Stewart Douglas

FAITH

Faith, laughing, bubbling, joyous faith,
In my ego, my country, in you
Faith lining the valleys with pure, crystal light
And the mountains with rich golden hue.

Faith, the nectar of all of the Gods,
One quaff and the currents that chill
Are gone from my life and the strength of your strength
Makes my weakness bow down to my will.

Faith, living, stirring, hoping faith
Faith that will lead straight and true
Faith in yourself, in your country, your friends
Will place you among the true blue.

Stewart Douglas
December 12, 1921

FATHER

I know a man who's battled life,
A conquering sort o' man,
Who neither loves nor fears the strife,
Nor seeks to lead the Van.
A man that every man must know
Where all good men foregather, -
Then clasp his hand and say hello,
His name, you know, is Father.

I know a man who's lost and won,
A rugged sort o' man,
Who sometimes looks beyond the sun
The deeper life to scan, -
The high ideal of tender youth,
A man who'll "Ride the River,"
Who builds his house upon the Truth, -
A gen'rous hearted giver.

I know a man who heads the race,
A steady sort o' man,
That marks of time are on his face, -
A part of Heaven's Plan,
A man who keeps behind the scenes,
Who's never in a lather,
Except when he has not the means
That brings joy to a Father.

So here's the thought that fills our heart
On this, our Father's day,
We'll make him feel that he's a part
Of everything that's gay.
We'll make this day of all the year
(The day that he would rather
Be something else than in his sphere)
The finest for our Father.

Stewart Douglas
May 14, 1931

FATHER'S KNOW TOO MUCH

The other night when I was Home
I didn't feel so good, --
Of course I'd lots of comforts,
Lots of things and lots of food.
But other things and other hopes
Were almost in my clutch, --
I looked at Dad and then found out --
THAT FATHER'S KNOW TOO MUCH.

It's awful sometimes just to feel
How Dads can be so firm!
Mother's eyes are soft as love,
But Dad's can make you squirm. --
And when you plan a wiener roast,
A ball game, swim, or such,
You look past Mother's smile and know —
THAT FATHERS KNOW TOO MUCH.

Of course, our Dads are awful good,
And I would be a Fool,
If I didn't recognize this truth,
They're Great Men as a rule.
But I hear my Daddy's echo say,
When Mother calls me Saint --
"Just try to be the finest boy
YOUR FATHER KNOWS YOU AIN'T".

Stewart Douglas

A FELLOW'S SISTER

I don't know how to take the news
It was me kind o' worried
But her it reads and straight from home
That Sister's getting married.
It sort o' cuts me up a bit,
For I shall often miss her
And I know there's no man good enough
For any fellow's Sister.

I don't know how you fellows feel
When news like this is carried,
But a fellow has a precious thing
In a Sister that's unmarried,
A precious pal he loves to tease,
And teasing loves to kiss her -
At heart there's no man good enough
For any fellow's Sister.

I suppose that I should celebrate
From morn 'till skies are starry
And lose no time but hasten back
Nor with my comrades tarry.
I know, I know, but yet I feel,
Tho I will sure assist her
No Prince or King's quite good enough
For any fellow's Sister.

Stewart Douglas

FEVERED

O' I want to make some money, and I want to make it quick,
Will you tell me how to do it, how to nimbly turn the trick;
It's a pile, I want to tell you, all the money I must have,
Can I make it, tell me plainly, and without the use of salve
For my conscience in the daytime, for my conscience in the night
And to soothe me into thinking I've been in an honest fight?
Can I make it, tell me truly, and I'll surely never kick?
But I've got to make it somehow, and I've got to make it quick.

O, money is not everything, I hear you theorize,
There are lots of folk with money you may heartily despise.
It may never bring the honey to the Honeysuckle Bee
But I'll bet it brings the honey to a simple chap like me.
How to make it clean and bravely, that's the thing I'm asking you,
I'm depending on your answer, make it honestly and true.
Is it work that you would answer - I've been working like old Nick,
Yet, I haven't found the answer that would bring me money quick.

I have had a living wage I know a score of years or more,
I have kept my home in comfort and a hospitable door,
But now I long to make my pile beneath the glistening sun,
Then will someone volunteer to tell me how the thing is done.
I've been careful, I've been thrifty - O, don't tell me to be true!
I still want to make some money, clean and quickly just like you, --
Ah! I thot you could not tell me 'though your thots are mighty wise,'
When you bring it down to "brass tacks", you can only moralize.

Well it seems I can't make money, I was fevered for a while,
I can only make a living in an ordinary style. --
You may make a thousand millions, you've the gift but I have not,
You may win a thousand battles while I may have only fought,
Yet I'll always feel the urge altho I cannot make it stick,
Just to make a pile of money and to make it bloomin' quick
-- What a glowing thrill 'twould give me if today I could but say,
"Here's a million for the fam'ly, let's go down the shining way".

Stewart Douglas

THE FINEST SIGHT

When a feller sees his little boy and girl linked arm in arm
And a toddlin' down the street to meet their dad,
With a smile upon their faces all his troubles to disarm
Why the Heavens seem to laugh and say they're glad.
And all the heavy weariness goes slipping off his back
And it seems that God is smiling on His throne
Just to see those little sweethearts climb and give him each a smack
Why a feller feels the world is all his own.

I tell you when a fellow's worked and sledged the whole day long
And he's feeling slow and heavy on his feet
There is nothing that will start the lilt and thrill him into song
Like the sight of those dear figures down the street.
With Mother in the doorway and their arms about him tight
Why a fellow's soul seems pillowed on the air
And a fellow's heart keeps praying that the Lord will keep him right
For the sake of those entrusted to his care.

Stewart Douglas

FOR AYE

We've squabbled, haggled, fought and fell,
And rose to fight again,
We've pierced each other through and through
With scourging words of pain.
We've quaffed the brimming cup of joy
Where fell the joyous sun,
We've tasted Heaven and tasted Hell,
And still we two are one.

We've sulked for days and sometimes weeks,
When lo! The ice would break,
And down the stream of love we'd glide
Relieved of ev'ry ache.
We've faced hard times when bread was scarce,
And work seemed never done,
We've run life's gamut just we two, -
And still we two are one.

I've laughed at her, made fun of her,
But kissed away her tears,
She's saddened me when I was glad,
But also calmed my fears.
We've hustled, tussled, toed the mark
And Pantingly we've run,
But yet with all our kindred faults,
FOR AYE WE TWO ARE ONE.

Stewart Douglas
May 19, 1931

A FRIEND IN NEED

A friend in need is a true friend indeed,
Is a maxim so true tho old
In the struggles of life, thru din and strife
Such a friend will never grow cold.

I have seen the sun in the spring of life
Rise gaily and gladsome and bright,
I've watched its radiance creep o'er the sky
And its glory was my delight.

But to see the sun of a friendly soul
And to feel its rich warmth again
Is something the glory of which transcends
The orb set in Heaven's domain.

I have seen the friends of the past grow cold
I have heard their laugh of disdain
When great misfortune o'er took me they fled
And left me to grief and to shame.

I've stood on battlefields close by a pal
Whose heart I then thought true as steel
But one night as I lay fast bleeding to death
He left me, false friend and unreal.

When you blacken your soul, when honor is dimmed
When you name is dragged in the dust
When friends you meet pass you on the street
Withering your heart with disgust;

When dark futurity marks out your fate
And you've fallen ever so low
Then you feel like the soul in Dante's refrain
So deep in the darkness below.

And the friends who in life's pleasant valleys
Were eager to follow your lead
In moments of darkness, pain and despair
Their cold backs have turned on your need.

Then something within rebels at the thought
Of true friends withholding their aid
And deeper you fall, revealed as you cry
"Will the love of the Lord thus fade?"

Thus it is ever dear friends in this sphere
In which we are called on to shine,
Of ten that were cleansed just one of them true
And now we ask "where are the other nine?"

It is not the man who when life's flowing fast,
Prosperity marking the way,
Stands by you and pats you, gives you sweet praise
Who'll stand by your side in the fray.

No! 'tis the man who in sorrow's dark hour,
When life becomes hard and you're sad,
When waves of sin beat 'gainst your storm-tossed life
Steps into the breach – makes you glad.

Glad by the fact that you know he's your friend,
That he's braved the world's scorn and hate
That his soul's been merged with your very own
And he's willing to share your fate.

He heeds not the world that bitterly cries
'gainst the wrong you've foolishly done
Loyal he stands by the friend of his youth
Imparting the warmth of the sun.

Such friendship as this, as rare as 'tis fine,
When you find it, cherish it well.
'Twill shine like a beacon lighting your path,
Its value none ever may tell.

For a friend in need is a friend indeed
'Tis a maxim new, never old,
In the struggles of life, thru din and strife
Such a friend will never grow cold.

Stewart Douglas

GETTING BY

If you are one who seeks to hide
Behind what is not you,
Then one day you will stand beside
A form that life will mock, deride,
Because it is untrue.
For none may ever build a wall,
To hide himself from one and all.

If you are one who hopes to do
With burnish'd tools of gold,
Some glittering task that may be new,
Some task that may be mighty too,
Where mighty throngs behold,
And leave the simple tools to rust
Your hope will scatter like the dust.

If you are one who just "gets by",
You'll find the signal's set
Against you both in earth and sky,
Though louder yours the battle cry
Than any uttered yet.
And gambling with such hapless stuff
The world will someday call your bluff.

Stewart Douglas

GIVEN THE LAUGH

The world's a waving field of truth
Meant for the sickle of age and youth -
And each one cuts his little patch,
Enough for his single roof to thatch.

Then finds his plotted corner bare,
And thinks he's captured the lion's share, -
But rich the grain waves on and on
Fuller at eve than at early dawn.

We all own plots and cast disdain
Over all the fields of uncut grain -
Great knowledge ours – devoid of chaff -
The gods look on and the gods they laugh.

Stewart Douglas
June 15, 1927

GOD

God's sought behind the dusky Cloud,
And not behind the blue-------
The multitudes will seek for bread,
He's worshipped by the few.

Stewart Douglas

GOD EVERYWHERE

How blind the sight, alas! How blind,
That does not see God stand reveal'd
And dark as night the light of mind
That anywhere God fails to find
By homely hearth or far afield.

Engraved upon the sacred dust
His holy name is plainly seen,
And deep into Earth's aged crust
Are writ the signs that all may trust
In every place where man has been.

No day that does not sound the word
Wherever man has planned or trod,
That does not show He is the Lord,
And that the ether sends this chord
The world's immersed in God.

Stewart Douglas

GOOD BOOKS

No matter where you wander and no matter where you look
You'll never find a friend so true and faithful as a book –
So faithful in the sunshine – filling moments when it's drear
With solace, joy and comfort and a brimming cup of cheer ; -
With the living thoughts that flow from every gifted pen,
Leading us to heights that tower above the sons of men. –
To glimpses of those human thoughts that gleam along the road
And teach us that the words of men but clothe the thoughts of God.

Stewart Douglas

A GOOD INVESTMENT

If you would invest in a fortune,
Invest in a woman's smile,
'Twill inspire you more than a war tune
And help you across each stile -
On the ocean of life it's an isle, -
A wonderful, wonderful fortune,
The wealth of a woman's smile.

We mortals are lost in it's wonder,
Spectres dissolve in that smile,
The shadows of night fall asunder,
Heaven's revealed for a while, -
It's an oasis every mile, -
A thrilling, perpetual wonder,
The wealth of a woman's smile.

Stewart Douglas
May 6, 1927

HAD WE BUT KNOWN

Had we but known that death was near
A legion hands with sword and spear
Had driven the monster back
But with a stealth and craft unseen
He stole upon our hearts serene
And drove his fell attack.

We cannot tell - we never know
The method of this unseen foe
That fills the breast with fear.
We only know beneath this mask
God calls to yet a nobler task
Within a higher sphere.

Stewart Douglas

THE HIGHER WAY

Let me mingle with men, let me mingle for then
Shall my real self be nurtured and fed
With the solemn and gay – from the commonest clay
I shall learn much, far more than I've read.
My thoughts may take wings where the ether bird sings
Or deep dwell in the shade of some glen,
In my choice of a star gleaming near or afar
'Twill be found 'mid the concourse of men.

In the deep forest path, the rich aftermath
Of a season of labor and care
You may see in the trees as they swing to the breeze
Drinking in the pure life-giving air
The wonderful skill of an all-potent will
On the morning when God sang so sweet
When He planted the seed, thinking then of your need
And the carpet of leaves for your feet.

On a hill far remote, on its green verdant slope
With the quietness of peace all around,
With the vale at your feet, an Elysian retreat
In a measure mayhap you have found
God in and around though you hear not a sound
And the ether seems quiet as the dawn
When the pale, inner gleam, loves to dream on and dream
Of the substance when shadows are gone.

But I want to mingle with men for O then
I shall know of their sorrow and pain,
I shall share in the joys of the old men and boys
And each day shall bring me great gain.
I shall look into eyes with the blue of the skies
And my life shall become deep and broad,
For 'neath every skin, white gleaming within
I shall look on the image of God.

Stewart Douglas

THE HIGHEST KINSHIP

See them struggle upward, heroes of the poor
Never losing courage – life itself the lure
Sons of widowed mothers reaching mountain heights
Strength of God within them after many fights.

Moulded in privation – taught an honest code
Trained so very early to bear a heavy load.
For millions rest nor fame, only work and toil
Heroes of the workshop, heroes of the soil.

God is surely with you, upward is your goal
Yours to conquer hardship, yours to win your soul
You with whom the ages keep a lasting tryst
Yours to know and feel true kinship with the Christ.

Stewart Douglas

HOPE SUCCEEDS HOPE

Wrecked are your hopes, blasted your dreams
You stand in the glare of the truth,
Shattered as swift as the passing of time
Swift as the passing of youth
But hope succeeds hope and dream follows dream
In the endless succession of things
And the cup of life fills as quick as it drains –
Eternal's the source of its springs.

Gone are the blossoms that bloomed for an hour
Withered your Eden of flowers
Hushed are the songs that sprang from your heart
Filling and tuning the hours
But the soil isn't dead and the flowers leave their seed
And a song that's been sung never ends
And a life that has tasted the deeps of true joy
Will again drain the joy that it sends.

Stewart Douglas

I SHALL NOT THINK OF DEATH

I shall not think of death, not now nor never.
Though phantoms from the ageless aeons past,
Come sweeping down, my hope of life to sever,
Or spectral shadows on my footsteps cast.
I shall not think of those who've gone before me,
What right have I to speak of fleeting breath?
I'll live! I'll live! The spell of life is o'er me,
I shall not now nor ever think of death.

I shall not think of death when life surrounding,
Speaks Joy and Lift, to heart, and soul, and brain.
When every moment brings me life abounding,
And from the seed I'm given golden grain.
I shall not think of death not now nor never,
Nor weep the time knew my soul no more.
Death's but a phantom – Lo! we live forever,
And reach its best when death throws wide the door.

Stewart Douglas

IF THE SUN ALWAYS SHONE

We love the rise of the peaceful morn
And the hour when the day is done,
But how should we fare with the constant light,
And how should we fare if the sun
Should never go westering down in the sky,
Should glare thru the days and years –
For what were the light if the night didn't come
And where were our joy without tears?

What were the world without shadow or cloud,
But desert and desolate waste?
How would a man know the shape of his soul
If danger he never had faced?
Where were the peaks of the high mountain range
If the valleys below were not there?
Where were the peaceful emotions of man
If mortals had never a care?

So we love the night for the change it brings,
We welcome the clouds and the rain.
The shadows are ours: but so are the flowers,
And strength follows weakness and pain.
After night comes the day, after day comes the night,
And care runs ahead to our sorrow,
A joy and a tear, a laugh here and there -
As we travel along to the morrow.

Stewart Douglas

INTERDEPENDENTS

For ourselves we may slip if we want to,
We may take it both easy and cool,
We may paddle our own away or at home,
We may act like the seer or the fool.
But there enters another equation,
An equation we cannot let pass;
We are only attendants and interdependents,
We are only a part of the mass.

If life were a common lone highway
Where only ourselves had to step,
There might be excuse for living life loose
And for losing our vigor and pep.
But now there's no room for evasion,
On us all now the rest sure depend;
Let each then be fervent and each man a servant
For this is life's goal and its end.

Stewart Douglas

INTERROGATION

What right have I of equal means with you
To pay the heavy price, while you go free?
Or why should you the heavy storms encounter,
While I go sailing down a placid sea?

What right have I to spare myself the trials
That you will meet unflinching to the end?
What right have you to walk through the vales enchanting,
While I unhappy trudge without a friend?

What right have you of equal means with me
To sit in peace, where better men have striv'n?
Or why should I be numbered with Gomorrah,
While you, without the price, step into Heav'n?

Stewart Douglas

THE ISSUES OF LIFE

I asked of the living world whence
Were the issues of life. In suspense
I awaited the answer. 'Twas given -
"They're not in the archives of Heaven,"

"Nor hid with the slumbering dead,
Whose spirits are farther ahead.
And not in a breed or a caste
Nor wrapped in the dust of the past."

"Go look!" came the answer intense,
"Go look!" with the clear eye of sense
The issues of life are not hidden
Nor are they to any forbidden.

I strove with my might to obey,
I strove in the clear light of day,
I seemingly strove in the strife;
Yet, - whence where the issues of life?

And I looked in the distance for God,
I tried every highway and road,
But wherever I went, 'twas despair,
For He seemingly never was there.

The shoes for a bare footed boy
Brought me the first taste of joy.
And I handed a widow her rent -
And down to me Heaven was sent.

And I helped an old man with his load
And out of the distance came God,
And he smiled with a smile that was fine -
Now God blends his labors with mine.

Stewart Douglas
Read at 1st Baptist Church, 1937

IT'S A GIFT

You've a college education fit for any situation,
According to the mood you now express,
And in football you're a wonder, you look it too by thunder,
Your character we know it by your dress,
You've swallowed Greek and Latin, you're versed in old Manhattan,
You've been in dear old Boston we can tell,
You're the kind we've been seeking , of whom we've just been speaking,
But, here and now's the question, can you sell?

You've the earmarks of a drummer, you ought to be a hummer
With all that you have picked up in your course,
With letters to your credit and without a single debit,
In selling sure you ought to be a force.
But let me whisper to you, let it percolate all thru you,
There're gifts on which we hardly need to dwell, -
You're fitted for high station with your wonder education,
Still, here and now's the question, can you sell?

Stewart Douglas

IT'S UP TO YOU

It is not the world you need to fight,
Tho' the world won't fight for you,
Your task is a somewhat different one,
But it's one that you can do.
And no one else may do it,
No one else may hear the call –
And God stands there with a smile that's rare
Tho' a thousand times you fall.

It's not the forces without you,
That will help or keep you back,
Tho' where you live be a mansion,
Or the homeliest wayside shack.
It's only the tenant within you,
It's only the man on the throne,
Who can give you a start, encourage your heart
And bring you at last to your own.

It's you who must fight all the battle,
It's you who must strip for the race.
You may lose but the effort's a vict'ry
Not to try is the only disgrace.
Your task may loom big and gigantic,
But it's worth all the time you can give
You'll only get there by learning to dare –
By knowing just how you should live.

Stewart Douglas

JUDGEMENT

I sat in judgment in the hall
Where all vain mortals sit,
I tried the foibles of my friends
And thought them void of wit.

The loves and hates of other men,
These, these were tried and banned, -
My house, you see, was built on rock,
But theirs upon the sand.

The poor I scanned and put to route,
The rich I pierced with scorn, -
I saw the greying clouds of night
Rise from the gilded morn.

The purple - blooming slopes of life, -
I saw them in reverse, -
I said that I was perfect, but,
It proved me just perverse.

I leant full weight upon my house, -
It's your turn now to mock, -
I found 'twas built upon the sand,
My neighbor's on the rock.

And now farewell the judgment hall
Where all vain mortals sit, -
My perfect deeds, my perfect words,
And thoughts were void of wit.

Stewart Douglas

JUST YOU AND ME TOGETHER

The world was made for you and me,
Just you and me together,
Beneath a roof or on the road,
Pledged to any weather.
Up high or down, as fate decides,
Naught will our spirits tether,
The world was made for you and me,
Just you and me together.

The world was made for you and me,
Just you and me together,
We'll face the steeps with buoyant hearts,
Nor fear the regions nether.
And should the shadows dim our eyes,
Above us grow the heather,
We'll sport again some otherwhere,
Just you and me together.

Stewart Douglas

KEEP IN THE HARNESS

Don't rest your oars because the shoreline heaves in sight,
Let your stroke be just as steady when the twilight heralds night,
If you slacken but a moment you may pay the final cost -
In the currents near the shore line home-bound sailors have been lost.

Don't think because you've lived a very useful, helpful life,
You must rest now from your labors, from the turmoil and the strife,
For though your life counts three score years, remember still there's ten,
So cast the burdens off your back and shake your feet again.

Don't dream of ever giving up – peace does not come that way,
Be blithesome, happy, think of youth, make up your mind to stay.
And then although the twilight gently deepens into night,
You'll have set the course for others, you'll have fought a winning fight.

Stewart Douglas
December 28th, 1923

THE KINDLY DAY

The kindly day has come again
When into hearts of love and pain
There comes a kinship tender;
When from the lighted crystal morn
True fellowship again is born
'Mid poverty and splendor.

Stewart Douglas
December 10, 1925

KNOTS

There are knots in the wood but we cover them over,
There are twenty one knots between Calais and Dover.
There are negative Nots and horrible Don'ts,
And balky old mules in the toss of our Won'ts.
There's the slip knot of marriage and Nots for our good,
There are knots in the porridge they serve us for food.
Forget-me-nots plenty, and knots in our quilts
As plain as the legs of a Scotchman in kilts.
There are knotty old problems and girls who are naughty,
But think of the knots in the men who are haughty.
There are hundreds of knots but the thing's to conceal them
And fix them so well that we'll never reveal them.

Stewart Douglas

THE LARGER GOD

They held Him within their narrow walls
In the days of long ago,
And thought He was deaf to other calls
Where men passed to and fro.
And they bound Him tight to their narrow souls -
He was God of a single race,
And they knew Him not where His vastness rolls
In the echoless tracks of space.

And they built into their sculptured stones
The ego of former days,
And hearts were moulded and cast in bronze
By the wealth of vain displays.
And they taught their sons of an insular God,
Who was wrapped in a little sphere -
And the creeds have followed the self–same road,
And the insular God is here.

And God looks on and He sees the god
That rests in the heart of each,
And the councils in heaven's chambers broad
Review the things that we teach,
And written deep in the council's scroll
Are the records of witless mind,
That has sought to bind to its insular soul
The God of the unconfined.

Stewart Douglas
August 17, 1927

LEAVES

Blighted, crumbling, saddening leaves,
To beauty and usefulness lost
Yesterday the harp of the wind
Today to be trampled and tossed.
Hither and yon to be scattered,
Fragments to mountain and sea
Like the chilling detaching autumn
That comes to my friends and me.

Frosted, dusty bespattered leaves
Perished your honor and fled
Above you skeleton forms speak
Of a glory past and dead
 Of a ruthless law that follows
Mankind and the green-leafed tree
And without respect of persons
Must follow my friends and me.

Stewart Douglas

LESSONS

What mean these lights along the way
If not to take the place of day?
What means the shining lives of men
If not to place us now and then
On plains of higher thought?
Where in the light we view again
The things that God hath wrought.

What mean these crowded streets of life
If not to fit us for the strife?
What means this going to and fro
If not to make us live and grow
To that for which we're made?
The brotherhood of man and lo!
The fear of man allayed.

What mean these fated ups and downs? -
A day of smiles; a day of frowns.
What mean these songs so mixed with tears
If not to fit us for the spheres
That lie beside the dawn?
Where we shall find the faith that cheers
And keeps us plodding on.

Stewart Douglas

LIGHT OF CHRISTMAS

Shining on far distant shores,
Shining on our very doors,
Wheresoever men have sailed
Glows the light that never failed.
Golden light of endless love,
Symbol of the hearts above,
Brighter now than when 'twas born,
Shining through this Christmas morn.

Singing in the breaking day,
Golden etchings thru the gray,
Songs that ages long have sung,
Bells that ages long have rung,
Songs of every tongue and clime
Blending in this hour sublime,
Sweeter than when song was born
Singing through this Christmas morn.

Light of spheres and light of men
Gleaming star of Bethlehem,
Earth shall rise because of thee
To her highest destiny.
And adorn the gleaming road
Men shall glimpse the face of God
Luminous, for 'tis Hope that's born
With this crystal Christmas morn.

Stewart Douglas
December 16, 1927

LIKE SHIPS THAT SAIL

The ship that reaches port today
Must sail again tomorrow.
For other lands and other ports
Though storms may bring her sorrow.
From port to port her course is set
Against the winds prevailing,
Alert and trim from stem to stern
Because she keeps a-sailing.

And so, like ships that sail the seas,
Each port is but a landing,
We must away to other tasks
Within our understanding.
It may not be to other shores,
Nor over mountains scaling,
But we must always keep alert,
And always keep a-sailing.

Stewart Douglas

THE LURE AND THE BLESSING

What sets the pace for all manking?
The chase for gold.
What is it cheapens womankind?
The lure of gold.
What makes the cheek once robust, white?
What turns the day so oft to night?
What makes two friendly nations fight?
Soulless gold.

What is it makes the gentle, gruff?
The coars'ning gold.
What is it never yields enough?
Deceitful gold.
What is it rings yon doleful bell?
What made that Mother's boy to sell
His soul unto the deepest hell?
Damning gold.

What is it robs the night of rest?
Spectral gold.
What is it crimsons red the breast?
Tragic gold.
What is it fills the sacred stream
From yonder source so pure and clean
With filth that may be felt and seen?
Corruptive gold.

What is it pays the grocer's bill?
The needful gold.
What gives you many an auto thrill?
The pleasing gold.
What is it cheers the night and day
And chases many a cloud away
And after work brings joy and play?
The precious gold.

Stewart Douglas

MAKE IT SHORT

If you've anything to say, make it short,
If you've anything to play, be a sport,
Wind will bring a world to grief
Darn the floodgates of relief –
Lord of mercy make us brief –
Make it short.

Stewart Douglas

THE MASTER BUILDER PASSES ON

The Master Builder passes on –
His race so nobly run –
But leaves behind for all to see
His record 'neath the sun.
So fine and straight and true and just,
Alike to friend and foe.
His strength was such that only death
Alone could lay him low.

The Master Builder passes on
But only from our sight
For Lo! Beyond the pale there gleams
His presence on the height,
And if we catch the meaning of,
The gleam that here is shed,
We'll know he's with the living though
He seems among the dead.

The Master Builder passes on
But passes not to stay,
His presence here you'll find upon
The red, red rim of day
And tho' he's gone this cheers us now
And tempers ev'ry sigh –
Death may have laid him very low
But God has rais'd him high.

Stewart Douglas
August 18, 1927

THE MASTER PIPER

I listened, and lo! All the desolate spots
Of the world sprang into view.
Desolate valleys, and desolate glens
And desolate cities too.
And I heard the rush of a mighty wind
And the moan of bending trees
Yet thru it there fell with a rustle soft
The breath of an eve'ng breeze.

Then over the tumult and desolate glens
Descended a peaceful calm
And I lay in the arms of a melody sweet
Soothing my spirit with balm.
And the morning rose with a golden flush
And the Heav'ns became serene.
And the desolate places smelled of flowers
And the valleys turned to green.

But hark! Thru the peace and the flush of morn –
The tread of a mighty host,
An army is swinging and marching along –
The battle is won and lost.
A paen of joy, the shock of the charge
Ranks split in two by the jar,
The wail of a nation bereft of her sons –
A lilt for the glory of war.

But laughing and joying I'm marching along
To the lilt of martial strains,
When sudden and sharp falls the chill of night
And the curse of despot chains,
And over the landscape gathering clouds,
And over humanity storms,
Then the melody changes and round me stand
A myriad of spirit forms.

Once again, it sweeps - a torrential stream -
Anon 'tis a mother's fears -
It bounds to an angel's tremulous voice
Quivering and full of tears.
Then a softness covers the glens and hills,
Like the softest sorrow known,
And lifting it leaves me an altered man,
With the fear of death all gone.

But the melody stops and the world once more
Returns to the common-place.
And there in the heat of a glen there stands
A piper of pride and grace.
Clad in the Cameron plaid of the Scots
Exuding a conscious pow'r.
He has reached the very soul of the world
And left me a sacred hour.

Stewart Douglas

THE MEANING OF CHRISTMAS

Kindness beaming in every eye,
Brotherhood written across the sky,
Cottage and mansion in happy accord,
Fellowship gleaming in action and word.
Touches of friendship, fervid and rare,
Clearing of brows that're heavy with care.
Smiles that are tender and smiles that are true, -
Are those not the meaning of Christmas to you?

Tales being told 'round every hearth,
Tales deep with joy and rippling with mirth,
Mistletoe, holly and silver sheen'd trees
Telling the story that always will please.
Love in the heart and love in the home,
Light of His star for men who must roam,
The gift of Himself that so thrills us through, -
Are these not the meaning of Christmas to you?

Stewart Douglas
December 16, 1927

A MICHIGAN GIRL

Wherever you see her she'll carry the signs
Of beauty and grace and symmetrical lines,
Fairer in figure and features than most,
A wonderful sweetheart, surpassing each toast.
Whether in PARIS or BAGHDAD you meet her,
Whether in LONDON or FRISCO you greet her,
You'll find she's compounded of rose and of pearl,
This charming, young, debonair Michigan girl.

But not alone charming, she sparkles with life,
Whether as maiden, or matron, or wife;
Spend in her presence an aeon or two
And you'll think she's been only a moment with you.
Something to sing of, you'll find her a dream,
Something to dream of, to love and esteem –
And if she is found by the plain man or EARL,
No less than a QUEEN, - She's a Michigan girl.

Stewart Douglas
May 21, 1931

A MICHIGAN MAN

With joy in his heart wherever he goes,
To the poles to the East or the West
With a light in his eyes like his own summer skies,
With a kindness for all in his breast.
A spring to his gait, a lilt to his step,
Like a leader who keeps in the van,
In the daylight or dark he carries the mark
And the stamp of a Michigan man.

He has lived, you can tell, where the winters
Bring a hardness thru combat and strife,
By the square of his chin and his resolute grin,
You can see he's the master of life.
A song on his lips, a hymn in his soul,
And the spirit to do what he can,
You can tell by his face, his strength and his grace
He's a vigorous Michigan man.

Stewart Douglas

MICHIGAN WOODS

I have pondered so often in various moods,
On the charm and beauty of Michigan's woods,
And I've felt as a man will when down on his knees,
When I've stood in the twilight surrounded by trees –

Surrounded by emblems of strength and repose,
Emblems of poetry where every wind blows -
So, honk for the clear and wide open road,
But I'm for the woods and the footfalls of God.

Stewart Douglas
December 16, 1923

A MIGHTY PRESENCE

At last we reap the spoils of common sense,
We see the world and all for which it stands,
No longer do we falter in suspense, -
Achievement's graven deep upon the sands.
And there on each horizon of the day,
That they who run may read and understand,
Flash signals to the men who do and pray
And sense a mighty pow'r throughout the land.

A pow'r that gathers as the years advance,
Surpassing ev'ry legendary tale,
And lifts a growing world to join the dance,
And rides the seas in ev'ry lashing gale.
With wings of steel it spans the ocean wide,
It flings its arms around the raging streams,
And harnessing the mighty wind and tide
It flashes o'er the world its cheering beams.

It takes the common strength of but a man
And multiplies it here a thousandfold –
A flash! And lo his thoughts leap out to span
The Universe that never will grow old.
And up beyond the glitter of the stars,
And far beyond the pale and reach of sight
New worlds that place the common stamp on Mars
Swim into view and ravish with delight.

It lifts the burdens that a former age
Bowed down and wrinkled long before its time,
It sets the race upon a higher stage
And tutors man with all that is sublime.
It works the iron into plastic steels –
Our tables groan with loads of finer food,
And underneath the world it places wheels,
And over all, the Lord has written "Good".

It broaches ev'ry morn the rising sun,
Lays some new off'ring at the feet of day,
Blends industry and art and makes them one,
Creates a fount within the common clay.
It spreads the charm of swift and leisure hours,
Translates the script of ev'ry awkward pen,
Pours blessings on the Earth like summer show'rs
And opens vistas beyond our ken.

It emanates from chambered, secret thought,
From genius in the many walks of life, -
Surpassing wonders ev'rywhere are wrought
And glory mixes daily with the strife.
And here where men have lost and men have won,
This presence reaches upward and abroad,
And keeps the race in spite of all that's done
Still knocking at the secret doors of God.

Stewart Douglas

THE MINER

He enters the mine and the fear of the Lord
Lies deep in the heart of the miner.
Through the shadows and dangers he traces the hand –
The hand of the Master Designer.

Far from the sun and the soft colored grass
There comes to his soul an elation.
He's been down in the depths with big-hearted men
In touch with the Soul of creation.

Stewart Douglas

THE MISERY OF SIN

"Sin was, is, and ever will be the parent of misery." – Carlyle.

She stalks through the land, in the stillness of night,
And oft in the broad light of day,
Creeps into the mansion, the cot, and the shop,
Too often a life-time to stay.

Clad in the rage of repulsion and sin,
Her feet are bared to the cold;
Her sad eye reflecting the depth of her pain,
What sorrows those lips could unfold!

She reeks not of time, nor her age can we tell;
But her garment's as old as the hills,
Alike to all ages familiarly known
As precursor – forerunner of ills.

You may meet her at e'en, you may meet her at dawn;
On the broad walks of life or within
If you let her she'll follow you down to the grave;
And her name is The Misery of Sin.

Aye, she stalks through the land in the stillness of night;
And oft in the broad light of day,
Creeps into the mansion, the cot, and the shop;
Too often a life-time to stay.

Stewart Douglas

THE MISTS ARE LIFTING

The mists are lifting, lo! The hills
Sing out their glad refrain,
The golden eye of Heaven shines
And all is well again.

The doubts that clouded soul and mind
Are gone, forever gone.
And lo! The hills of light and truth
Rise from the soft'ning dawn.

The murky past lies far behind,
The highway gleams with light,
We tread the beckoning, forward shores,
Outside the mist of night.

Stewart Douglas
March 17, 1928

MONSTERS

Hurtling through the night
Ditches that affright
Blinding lights forever straight ahead
Wet the night or dry
Monsters rushing by
Gambling for a place among the dead.

Stewart Douglas

THE MOTHER OF MY BOYS

My life has kept a steady course thru every passing year,
My life's been given added force, because of you my dear.
I clasp you to my heart my love, you're all the world to me,
I owe my more than all dear heart, my more than all to thee.

Chorus
I cannot tell the world how much I owe you,
You've made me feel life's purest, sacred joys.
My heart is Thine, tho time should last forever,
And only Thine, dear Mother of my boys.

Life's thorns tho sharp can never harm, since you are with me dear,
Life's gilded path can hold no charm since you are ever near.
Your love has purified my life, refined it from all dross,
With all the world at my command without you 'twould be lost.

Stewart Douglas

MOTHER TO DAUGHTER

Our Daughter! Sweet, tender word.
How vain attempts to rank you!
How oft the heights for you we'd climb,
But – sometimes we could spank you.

Yet here's the hope that fills us men
And deeper binds each other,
May blossoms red your past bestrew,
Rich, redder than for mother.

Stewart Douglas

MOTHER'S DAY SONG
to the tune of "Danny Boy"

Oh, mother dear, the summer winds are saying,
The hills of home are crooning your dear name,
And you and I today will go a-maying
For, mother dear, you always are the same.
My whims and fancies always were your pleasure,
My fears were lost within the boundless flow
Of love that God alone could match or measure,
Oh, mother dear, Oh, mother dear you lov'd me so.

Oh, mother dear, were shadows o'er me lying,
The dews I'd know were but your crystal tears,
Were I within the shadow of the dying,
Your love would close the gate upon my fears.
That shall I say for love that's always spending
And never spent no matter where I go,
My feeble words for love that is unending,
Oh, mother dear, Oh mother dear I love you so.

Stewart Douglas

MUSIC

The Nightingale may charm your ear with sweet elusive song,
The Lark may lend its voice to the sublime,
And ever sweet harmonic chords to charm your soul along
You'll hear 'mong woodland elves from time to time.
But music, tho the songbirds cease in every wood or glen,
Shall come to me in rhythmic beat from the tender hearts of men.

The murmuring brook, the cataract, many touch your very mood,
The shimmering stars sing down their silver tones,
Your soul with mountain peaks may blend whereon you've often stood,
And God may teach you rhythm in the stones.
But notes entrancing, powerful, grand and great beyond our ken,
Come pulsing, flowing, cheering on, from the tender hearts of men.

So when I want to feel the surge and thrill of all the spheres,
Where laughing, bubbling, trilling lyrics flow,
I seek the busy haunts of men, the comradeship that cheers,
And find my heart attuned and all aglow, -
Attuned because I've touched the running, limpid stream again,
The gurgling stream of Life and Love from the tender hearts of men.

Stewart Douglas

MUTUALITY

Dear little diamond how I hate
To part with you again,
The hands that you have graced before
Would number almost ten.
And this dear hand I'm holding now,
Once more you are to favor, -
Dear little diamond make her see
How ardently I crave her.

I bought you when the price was low,
Two hundred's what I paid,
Since then you've brought the flush of joy
To many a handsome maid.
What's that you said dear girl of mine?
O yes, I love to linger
Within the circle of your love –
Slip this upon your finger.

Alas, dear little diamond mine,
You're gone, forever gone,
For thoughts escaped my lips one night
While dreaming of the dawn.
"Farewell," she said, you've told enough,
This ring to me you've given,
Will add one more to what I've got
And bring the count to seven.

Stewart Douglas

MY MICHIGAN HOME

Like the first deep spell of a lover's love
When the heart's so full, and the lips so mute,
When the red veins dance and the slow pulse leaps,
When the pure wine bursts from the luscious fruit -
Comes the silent charm of a gleaming night,
When I wordless stand 'neath this starlit dome,
Which God in a tender, beautiful mood,
Has plac'd just above my Michigan home.

Like the linger'ng charm of a woman's soul,
Like the linger'ng presence she leaves behind;
Like her fragrant life reaching far and near,
And carried afield on the passing wind, -
Comes the perfumed breath of a summer morn,
When the wild stag leaps at the call of day,
When the green slopes smile to the sun-kissed lakes
Where the soul grows strong and the spirit gay.

Like the nectar'd hills where I used to play,
In the old dear days of the summer time,
Like the brooding peace of the silent plains,
Like the blended joys of every clime, -
Comes a day with the rest o' the world forgot,
When the smiling acres I love to roam
Are under my feet, and I stroll content,
Where Heav'n shines down on my Michigan home.

Stewart Douglas

MY OLD TATTERRRED BOOKS

They're old and they're worn and they scarce hang together,
They've come through the years and through all kinds of weather,
They are ugly to look at, yet wealthy within
Like a true honest soul with a rough outer skin,
Yet they breathe out their message as fresh as the hour
When they first reached my heart with their singular power,
They're my best friends and faithful, whatever their looks,
For the staff of my life is my old tattered books.

They clutter my shelves yet I do not care whether
They take from the looks of the books bound in leather,
My heart's in these old tattered volumes of mine
For I've read and re-read them line upon line.
Tho scattered the leaves and tho faded the print
They are rich in their utterance beyond any mint
For when weary, I rest by the meadows and brooks
When I browse for an hour thru my old tattered books.

Stewart Douglas
August 10, 1931

MY WISH

Some friends who understand me and may yet remain my friends,
A work to do of value and the rest that each task sends,
A work that shall not burden those who mete out my reward,
But done so well that every day shall merit their regard.
A mind that's unafraid to scan a past that can't be praised
Or travel into unknown paths long ere the trail is blazed.
A heart that understands each heart and beats and blends with all,
And gladly risks a pain or ache to answer every call.

A sense of humor deep within, and the hearty power to laugh,
This, of all the means of life, its strongest, surest staff,
A little leisure left to me to meditate on truth,
And the power to take advantage of the eager days of youth. –
A touch of the eternal strength that lies beyond the hills,
And the will to pass it on to counteract another's ills. –
A sight of the unresting sea, its turbulence and roar --
These will bring the throb of life a-pulsing to my door.

Stewart Douglas

THE NEEDS OF THE HOUR

The world needs the brilliant, the polished and famed,
Her sons who by greatness (the god) have been named,
Her leaders of masterly tactics and mind
Are now in demand from before and behind,
But each day with force and intensified power
Comes the press and the need and the urge of the hour,
For men who to duty are harnessed and ready
Men rock-ribbed, unswerving, dependable, steady.

The millionaire (multi) perhaps the world needs,
And men acclaimed heroes of outstanding deeds,
True statesmen of conscience and Captains with sand
With the grit of conviction are still in demand.
But out of the world there's a cry going forth
That extends to the south, the east, west and north,
For men who are girt with the truth ever ready,
Men rock-ribbed, unswerving, dependable, steady.

True Captains of commerce and men who are leal
The world values highly because they are real.
These big men of business with big honest hearts,
These men who are leaders in all the world's marts,
These men have spoken, proclaimed with one voice
For the needs of the hour they have only one choice –
'Tis bound up in this, in the men girt and ready
Men rock-ribbed, unswerving, dependable, steady.

Stewart Douglas

THE NEW DAY

Old things shall pass with the year that is dying,
Old grudges, old doubts and old fears.
The days that we spent in our folly and sighing
Shall pass with the days that we spent full of tears
And passing beyond all our skill to recall them,
The days that were dark and the days full of loss,
The new day now comes with a tread almost solemn
And holds in its hand both a sceptre and cross.

New things shall come with the year that is breaking,
New hopes, aspirations, new songs.
New courage to keep to the big undertaking,
The bearing of burdens, the righting of wrongs.
The new day now dawns for the young and the olden,
The outgoing tide with it carries the dross;
It stands on the threshold with offering golden,
And holds in its hand both a sceptre and cross.

Stewart Douglas

NO SUBSTITUTE

Modest little maiden see
All the world is full of thee
Turn me whereso'er I will
There I find your potent thrill.

In the market or the den
In the living haunts of men
There unseen your face I view
I must be in love with you.

Modest little blushing girl
All my thoughts are in a whirl
Now the cause of all my pain
Since you've said me nay again.

Blushing little maiden fair
Golden sunlight in your hair
Filtering every shaft of light
For your smile I'll live and fight.

Tender hearted, pure and whole
Heav'n has bless'd your crystal soul
Yet Heav'n has nothing else to give
If from your side I'm forced to live.

Stewart Douglas

ODE TO KIPLING

If I should choose between these men,
If I had but one choice,
'twixt Eddie Guest's or Kipling's pen,
Then listen to my voice.

I'd rather be like Eddie Guest
Than be in Kipling's bed.
It's not a question which is best –
For, --Rudyard Kipling's dead.

Stewart Douglas

ONLY A QUARTER

When he dropped it in as I passed the hat
To pay for the doctor's fee,
That saved old Ned from the stony stare
And an uphill climb, you see. –
When he dropped it in as I've said before,
His gaunt frame slightly shook,
But his eyes lit up with the sparkled light
That comes from a silvered brook.

When he dropped it in as I've now said twice,
He slipped from the giving crowd,
A stranger to all – never seen before,
Not too well-dressed but proud.
But I thot of him not as he left us there
Where we counted the money for Ned,
'Till the moon went down and I stumbled across
The stranger's grassy bed.

He'd been thru the mill, thru the scorching fire,
He knew just the feelings of Ned.
'Twas only a quarter he dropped in the hat,
'Twas all that he had he said.
And my heart welled up at his simple words,
And I thot of the ways of God,
How the kindness of hearts will rise to the top,
In spite of the lash and rod.

I have passed the hat many times since then,
But nothing can give me the thrill
That a quarter gives when it jingles against
The brim of a hat, or till.
Only a quarter, the stranger had said,
A quarter with meaning so fraught!
When it's all you have with nothing in sight
A quarter's a "HELLUVA" LOT.

Stewart Douglas

OPPORTUNITY

Opportunity comes, to one and all
And its portals fling back wide,
And it sends its challenging voice and call
Where the souls of men abide.
'Tis heard in the depths, and the highest height
Where wandering men have fared,
But answered alone in the conscious might
Of the men who are prepared.

Opportunity comes, 'tis marked and known
In all the walks of men,
Marked by the seed you have daily sown
In the valley or the plain.
It comes in stealth or with clarion voice,
Its message alone is heard
By the men who sweat in the field of choice,
By the men who are prepared.

Stewart Douglas

O WHAT A GOOD OLD WORLD

I stood on the threshold – the dawn of day fair –
With my eyes eastward turned to the sun,
There were pearls on the lily and wine in the air,
Bringing joy ere the day's work begun.
I drank to the full of that life giving air
And my voice to the breezes I hurled,
"I'm glad I'm alive", and the echo came back,
Oh! – O what a good old world!

I stood in the broil and the heat of the day,
And the lily had withered and died.
Some bore well the heat with ne'er a complaint
While others oft grumbled and sighed.
And then came a rain-laden cloud o'er the sun
And the hissing wind whistled and whirled,
And again on the winds went the cry of my soul,
Oh! O what a good old world!

I stood once again with the westering sun
Sinking low on the rim of the sky.
My body now ached from the toil of the day,
And for rest would incessantly cry.
And glancing ahead to the hour of my rest,
'neath the covers I snugly lie curled,
I have still this to say whether here or away,
Oh! O what a good old world!

Stewart Douglas

THE PARAMOUNT QUESTION

It's neither the place where a man was born,
Nor the day or date of his birth,
These only show that he's living down here,
A citizen merely of Earth.
The thing that counts most and will gain for him more,
Howsoever your argument's based,
Is not when and where he arrived on the scene
Nor why – but how was he raised?

It's neither tradition nor family name,
Or the pride of a long honored line,
These may be worthy when given their place
And may help a man some of the time.
But the thing that may point to a lasting defeat,
Or a strength that shall never be fazed,
Is the question that rises above all the rest, -
Just how was the gentleman raised?

Stewart Douglas

PARENT OR FATHER?

Does your boy look up in faith to you?
Is he happy when by your side?
Does he love to show you off to his crew?
When he does, does he do it with pride?
If not, you must think – to be callous you daren't –
From the thot of the world you will gather
A man may have all the claims of a parent
And never be classed as a father.

Do you give your boy the kind of advice
That will thrill him in after life?
When he's needing the pep to get at the spice –
When he's breasting the currents of strife?
If not, you will wish that a parent you weren't,
When your lad comes to you in a lather
And finds he's been trusting his all to a parent
Who could not be classed as a father.

Stewart Douglas

A PARTY FEELING

When a party feeling fills you up don't squelch it on a bet.
Go out and call the neighbors one by one,
Throw out your chest and show them you're as young as they are yet.
Forget your years and have a little fun.
Get round the old piano till the joys of olden times
Goes coursing – rushing thru your every vein,
Till heart and soul are dancing with the old melodious chimes,
And stripping off the years, you're young again.

A party feeling beats all else for keeping old men young.
When'er it bubbles o'er you it's a sign you're not among
The "has beens" or the Edgar Allan Poes.
But if you've never had it and your thoughts are often blue
And those around you think you're but a crank,
Just send the invitations tho they'll scarcely think it's you,
And you'll find you're putting something in the bank.

Stewart Douglas

PASSING

The staid old minds of the staid old days
With their old time lofty inspiring ways
Are passing as passes the summer breeze
When Autumn is stripping the leaves from the trees,
And the world shall miss them – the world of men
From the highlands, the lowlands, the city and plain,
But the faith they have kept and the course they have run
Shall live till the light flickers out of the sun.

So passes the old days so rich and serene,
So passes the hours when we found time to dream
Now if we find time to sleep we do well
In this hustling, bustling, premature Hell.
But somehow we like it, this bustle and roar,
Our blood must run faster than ever before.
But let us tho loving the life that is fast
Draw deep from the strength of the days that are past.

Stewart Douglas

PASS ON

Pass on old friend, you've stood by me
Far more than I by you,
You've done your bit throughout the world
Where bells are ring'ng true;
And though you bear the scars of strife
This cannot be your end,
For down the years that loom ahead
I'll call you still my friend,
For thoughts that came if not to me,
To bless the hours of those,
Who needed more than you or me,
The solace of repose,
Then pass -- I'll meet you otherwhere,
Without a sigh or tear,
Meanwhile I'll swear allegiance
To your offspring, the NEW YEAR.

Stewart Douglas
12-27-26

PERPETUAL VACATION

Perpetual sunshine would not do
Perpetual rain would drown us
To look forever on the blue
Would silence, seal, and crown us
Perpetual work from morn till night –
Alas! Our souls revealing
Would be a constant uphill fight,
Unsought and unappealing.

Despite the words of wiser men
Perpetual wealth would suit us,
We swear we'd be in bed at ten
And nothing would uproot us
But there is something else, it seems,
Would bring the most elation
The answers to our fondest dreams,
Perpetual vacation.

Some choose the snows, a splendid time,
Good winters will not freeze us –
Some love the fall and spring sublime
And these would blithely please us.
The choice of June will often bring
Many a bright oration
But give us summer, winter, spring
And fall for our vacation.

Stewart Douglas

A PRESENT FOR A WEDDING

A happy road you're starting on,
A happy road to travel,
Macadamized for many miles,
With here and there some gravel.
But rough or smooth the going's fine,
Just starting you'll not rue it,
What you're about to do, dear friend,
We all would love to do it.
So here's to you and here's to her,
While moons grow full or crescent, -
The hope that you may reach the best
Explains this little present.

Stewart Douglas

THE PRISON

Into the City, the City, I strode,
The metropolis great of the West,
Where humanity seething
With no time for breathing,
Lay clutched in the maw of unrest,
And straightway the prison engulfed me
The walls rising sheer on each side –
Into the City, the City, I strode,
Away from the City I'll ride.

Into the City – O pity – I strode,
Between its unscalable walls
Where the noise as of battle,
Of peace, the death rattle –
'Twere better to live in the stalls.
The City –where sparrows grow sickly,
Where a night will your freshness decay, -
Into the City – O pity, I strode,
In the morning I'm riding away.

Into the City – at noontide, I strode,
Where the pallor of death on each face
Showed its grim stony soul
Beyond human control,
In the morning my steps I'd retrace.
Back with the grasses, the big friendly trees,
Back where the birds trill so gay,
Into the City at noontide I strode,
In the morning I'm speeding away.

Stewart Douglas

THE QUEST

I stood beside a stranger in the far off frozen North
In a land where silence marks the great unknown,
He was fleeing from the sordid, he was seeking the sublime,
And wist not he'd have found it back at home.
How dry indeed and barren must the life of that man be
Who, seeking the sublime must scour the Earth,
When here amid the children's smiles and happy laughing glee
The sublime is circling all around his hearth.

I stood beside a stranger in the sunny south of France
In a land that's matchless for its balmy clime,
He was seeking, so he told me, that elusive thing of life,
The elusive super thrill of the sublime.
How often have I pondered and often wondered too
Why men will search the world from shore to shore,
When that for which they're seeking in its finest perfect form
Maybe found sublime inside a neighbor's door.

Again in thought I stood beside the hills of Galilee
Two thousand years, of course, before my time,
Where people had been trained to keep a lookout for their prince,
Whose coming would be kingly and divine.
And when he came with humble mein, with soft and kindly eye,
Around the hills, along the dusty road
They did not see the splendor nor discover the sublime,
Yet they looked upon the counterpart of God.

And so my simple message I would pass along to you
The sublime is not beyond the rim of Earth,
But here and there and everywhere on sea and shore and sky
But only as you recognize true worth.
In the simplest of life's aspect, in its crudest, coarsest form
I would press this truth, of course it isn't new,
You will always find a touch of the sublime in man or worm,
Or the world will fail to find it, friend, in you.

Stewart Douglas

THE REAL AMERICAN

It's fine to see a man declare intentions
And then allegiance to our country swear,
To snap forever all his old conventions
And feel that he is better here than there.
But something here you'll grant to me is needed
Than this in you or me or any man,
His vice by virtue must be superseded
Before he'll make a true American.

It's finer still and far beyond contention
And here I know again you will agree,
To see a man with clear-cut comprehension
Trace back and hand you down his pedigree.
It may be spotless and it may be splendid
For generations back perhaps it ran,
But if his own life cannot be commended
He's not a "Simon-pure" American.

It's not alone the oath above I mention
Nor yet how good the stock from which you came
That'll focus on you any one's attention
In words of praise, of censure, or of blame.
But what are you? Our country seeks an answer.
Have you breathed her truth – the essence of a man,
Is your life the kind of life that will enhance her
If it is you are a real American.

Stewart Douglas
February 20, 1922

REAL LOVE

She came into my life one day,
I know not what possessed me,
Something warm and near divine
Instantly caressed me.
Her eyes, I knew not what their hue,
Her hair I had not noted,
But suddenly the skies were blue
And I stood there transported.

Since then the common ups and downs
Have come to me nor missed her,
But back the clouds have always rolled
Each time my lips have kissed her.
How I had lived in days remote
Ere I had thought about her
God only knows for now I know
I could not live without her.

Stewart Douglas

THE REMEDY

Have you heard the latest order skimming clear across the border?
Buckle down and face the future without fear.
'Tis a day and hour for action when each unit – every faction
Must get down to solid business and cohere.
'Tis an hour when heavy grading must be done by heavy spading,
When our coats must all be thrown off to a man,
When we all must hitch together and stay hitched despite the weather –
Well I can't conceive of any better plan.

Have you seen the latest headlines how to shorten up our breadlines?
And to save ourselves from everlasting shame,
We must recognize each other on the common ground of brother
And get back to human principles again.
We must leave behind the slouches at the same time ditch our grouches
And let by-gones sleep or slowly, quietly die,
Then begin concerted action which will bring true benefaction
And the hearts of honest men will satisfy.

Stewart Douglas

RICHES

The fetters snap, the day is done,
Forgotten the ragged strife,
And the homeward goal
Has heaven in the soul
For the man with a smiling wife.

Mellowed and rich, joyous and glad,
Bubbling with laughter and life,
He stands in the sun
And all things have come
To the man with a smiling wife.

Stewart Douglas

THE RIVER OF LIFE

I've tasted it, drank of it, plunged in it too,
And swam thru the heart of it, loving it true,
I've countered its currents and swept on its breast
From the rim of the east to the rose tinted west.
I've waded its edge like a boy in his teens
And rowed on its silver sheened surface of dreams,
And I've cared for it least, yet it held for me more
When it forced me to labor and bend to my oar.

I've drifted along, but tho strange it may seem
In the end I've been happier pulling up stream,
And you'll find this will always be true in your case
No matter what mask life may wear on its face.
When the currents are sweeping with strenuous might
Just bend to your oars in the darkness or light,
Point your bark up the stream and lay a true course
Up the River of Life and you'll come to its source.

Stewart Douglas

THE ROAD TO BETHLEHEM

Come with me now to Bethlehem, it is not very far,
The road is short and easy and illumined by a star, -
A star that in my troubles gives again the will to smile,
And another bit of courage to try the second mile.
Come, join me in the journey for it won't take very long, -
It's just around the corner, and, wherever men have trod,
The road that leads to Bethlehem is on the road to God.

Let's look within the lighted homes where men and women are,
And walk along the lighted streets, well lit by lamp and star,
Let's look to where life's crosses dim and glowing, ancient light, -
Let's change the darksome Calv'ries to Bethlehems tonight.
For God would join the souls of all on this immortal day,
And light the path of every man who gives his heart away
To friendship, love and service in narrow field and broad, -
And that's the road to Bethlehem, and that's the road to God.

Stewart Douglas

ROAD TO THE STARS

"I'd love to sit where the stars shine high,
Above Earth's cares and fears,
I'd love to talk with the tall, high souls
Whose works have adorned the years,
But well I know that the road to the stars,
As I handle this wayward pen,
Lies not in the heights I'd love to reach,
But – down in the valleys ----with men."

Stewart Douglas

ROOSEVELT

Roosevelt – nor age, nor clime has ever bred a greater,
Loved by many, feared by some, and honored by his Maker.
Born a weakling in a hour when men demanded Iron,
Yet conquering every ill that strove his body to environ.
Struggling on through thick and thin with sickness often taunted,
Climbing up the rugged hill with courage all undaunted,
Reaching to the highest peak that may be reached by man,
His name now shines in hist'ry as "The First American."

Stewart Douglas

ROYALTY

A truthful man's an honest man,
An honest man's a Peer,
They each have rugged qualities
That cannot live with fear.
A humorous man's a mighty man –
He holds an honored place,
But a loyal man's a royal man –
The King of every race.

A tactful man the world applauds,
And men who set men free,
And men who serve their fellow men
Wherever men may be.
The lover and the old-time friend –
Their praise shall be a flood,
But a loyal friend's a royal friend
Of Heaven's bluest blood.

Stewart Douglas

THE SAGINAW RIVER

It has not the on-rush of cataract streams,
Nor is it a river you'd see in your dreams;
It has not the murmur that lulls you to sleep
Like shallower waters that flow to the deep.
Few poets have sung it in these busy days,
It flows without tribute, it flows without praise, -
But O! What an epic of passion and might
The Saginaw River might easily write.

It may not have charm as it courses along,
It may not give echoes of music and song;
But forests have swam on its turbulent breast
While souls were unbared to the ultimate test.
And Grit rode its bosom unflinching and bold,
And laughed in the face of life's perilous hold,
While men were remolded and cast in the raw,
When measuring strength with the old Saginaw.

It may not have beauty in all of its length,
But rugged old men still speak of its strength.
Its banks may be bare and ungraceful in line,
But once they were guarded with Michigan pine.
It may be a common old river 'tis true,
Holding no interest at present for you,
But O! If its secrets should unfold tonight,
What an epic the Saginaw River might write.

Stewart Douglas

SAME OLD

It's the same old sun, the same old moon,
    And same old sky above us;
It's the same old roads, the same old modes,
    But the same old friends that love us.

It's the same old thoughts, the same hopes,
    And the same old scenes that bore us;
The same old jokes, but the same old folks
    And the dear ones that adore us.

It's the same old pain, the same old aches,
    And the same old sins that hire us;
The same old flowers, the same old show'rs,
    And the same old smiles that cure us.

It's the same old seed, the same old field,
    And the same old doubts that sear us;
The same dark night, but the same white light
    And the same old songs that cheer us.

Stewart Douglas

A SAVING REMEMBRANCE

Tho' the long years have passed I can still see his face
As he sat by the old front room fire,
And tho' sleeping the sleep of the blessed, I know
That his image will always inspire.
Tho' wrinkled his features and scanty his hair,
And with sometimes a look that was sad –
Oh! I'll carry the thot that of him deep in my soul –
The living remembrance of Dad.

Tho' oceans divide from his last resting place
His memory never will fade;
Discouragement flees when I think of his smile –
A smile the dear Lord must have made.
When bitterness lurks and would strike at my heart,
When I'm tempted and "all to the bad,"
There flashes before me that picture of life –
That saving old picture of Dad.

Stewart Douglas

SAY IT NOW

You'll speak of him gently for many a day,
You'll tell of the wisdom he had,
Of the deeds of his life and his hatred of strife –
You'll recall where he played when a lad.
You'll speak of the people he helped when he could,
How he stood for the right when alone,
But you'll silent remain thru the sunshine and rain
'Till after the loved one has gone.

You'll deck him with flowers in a beautiful way, -
The thoughts they express are sublime,
But had they been said ere your dear friend was dead,
How happy for him and how fine.
Oh to speak out the word giving courage and cheer
That will help a friend forward and on! –
If you've garlands to give you will happier live,
If you give them before he is gone.

Stewart Douglas

THE SCOURGE

From what heights of eminence have you not
Looked down on the feeble attempts of man
To reach you, O Scourge of the Soul. In the
Clouds enshrined, in your own domain secure,
At humanity's attempt to find you
You have laughed. Height after height the sons of men
You have led to scale, and they, from the high
Pinnacles of achievement, have dizzy
Grown and weary in the futile attempt
To go farther. In your lofty, lofty
Habitation man has placed you, little
Dreaming as the years rolled on that more and
More unattainable and unscaleable
Would the path to that habitation grow.

He forgot, as he now forgets, that true
Success was ever near and closely linked
To the human race. He forgot that the
Happy fireside was your abode, forgot
That in the eyes of the workman you gleamed
Brightest at the end of a well-done tack –
Forgot that the menial task done in the
Right spirit is the acme of success.

But now it requires the utmost energy
To spur us on. To reach you our whole soul
Is spent in vain. Each year finds you farther
Removed. The tyranny of oppression
Is nothing to the toll you exact. For
Generations the undaunted have almost
Reached you, only by your cunning to be
Eluded. Still you beckon them on, and
Onward they go. Multitudes find their locks
Whitening and their shoulders stooping in
Their mad endeavor to reach you. How you
Have deluded the sons of men! What guilt

Seems wrapped in your very shadow!
What stories of gaunt, haggard faces and
Shriveled lives could you not tell! The future
Holds nothing in your favor. Whither will
You lead today's aspiring throngs? Onward
And upward towards your cloud-capped pinnacle?

Yes, onward and upward, only at their
Approach to withdraw yourself higher, to
Remain far enough from their grasp to taunt
Them – only to see on the faces of
Countless men after a life of struggle
To reach you, the receding light of hope
And glory – the succeeding grey of chill
Disappointment and despair. Only to
See them standing on the pinnacles you
Have formed, with the waves of memory
Lapping their feet, and the burden of the
Years pressing them down – only to watch them
With a feeling of elation in your
Unconscionable soul – only to mock
Them as their souls are dissolving in the
Cauldron of bitterness; only to wait
The opportune moment when you may flood
The valley (the valley to which, the seeing,
They may nevermore descend) with a light
Revealing, as only to hopeless, homeless
Men it can be revealed, the peaceful scenes
Far below, the dotted hillsides, the bright
Faces, happy smiles, and contented homes.

Stewart Douglas

SHALL WE CHANGE OUR PLAN

A great many things have been done for the race
Since the day that creation began
By elegant masters and strict Zoroasters
For the help and perfection of man.
Laymen and yeoman have tried every means
What consummate arts they employ
But eminent teachers may go to the "Bleachers"
Unless they begin with the boy.

Despite what we've done tho it may be our best
Our best for the welfare of man
Men still are falling swift, sure and appalling
For want of a happier plan.
Big men and great men are giving their talents
To tasks that we all now enjoy,
But we can't make our nation the peak of creation
Until we begin with the boy.

Stewart Douglas

SHIFTING THE BLAME
Written during the Great Depression

For everything on land or sea wisdom finds a cause,
Except when fierce depression prowls the Earth;
We scan with scanty merit both our plain and mystic laws,
To find the meaning of the fireless hearth.
But after all our jargon, like a rush of wind at night,
Like pictures of a path way never trod,
We shift the heavy burden and we think we've found the light.
By charging the depression up to God.

For crime and greed and folly we can find a reason true;
We measure suns and planets in their course,
We know why verdant nature's green and why the sky is blue, -
We calculate the pow'r of any force;
But economic blunders that consume the souls of men,
And bows the world beneath an awful load,
Have far too many answers so with one accord and pen,
We charge the cruel matter up to God.

Charge nature's twist to Mother, Ah! But not to motherhood,
Or trace it back a hundred years or more;
Charge poverty to Brethren, Ah! But not to brotherhood, -
The word's a mere misnomer on our shore.
For wheat is fed to cattle while our bread-lines we enlarge,
The jobless tread the long and thorny road. –
It's distinctively ungodly for anyone to charge
The guilt of all humanity to God.

Stewart Douglas

THE SILVER SIX

I've found the car I envy, I've been in the "Silver Six",
It's a whirlwind, it's a greyhound, it's a bird.
It is fit for any creature, it has ev'ry kind of feature,
To describe it I am short the fitting word.
And its comfort? (It's a Buick) I lie awake at night
Gently dreaming of the car that takes all tricks.
For ev'ry kind of drummer here's the car that is a hummer,
It's the racing, pacing, gracing "Silver Six."

I've found the car I venture I may some day own myself,
In its make-up it's the only lasting kind.
It is perfect in its gearing to its throttle and its steering
And its passengers may ride with ease of mind.
If I only had the "wherewith" I'd quickly run and buy.
But alas! The lack of money is my fix.
But as sure as bees make honey, you'll be losing more than money
If you buy before you view the "Silver Six".

Stewart Douglas
August 6, 1928

SMILING MICHIGAN

What kindly land is this old part that you and I have found?
Where all's serene and friendly folks on every hand abound,
Where sunny days and starry nights and time just rolls along,
   And life can only be expressed in bubbling, merry song.

What magic land is this old friend, or have I dreamed a dream?
Of restful nights and cooling winds and slumber deep, supreme,
Where starlight's soft and smiling hope's the symbol of the sky,
A land of singing streams and lakes where one could live and die.

What homey land is this old chum that lies in calm repose?
Beneath the gilded, vaulted heights, beside the scented rose,
Where quickened pulses beat with joy and eyes are turned above,
Where deeper runs the channel of the hearts that are in love.

See! There upon the flushing morn just breaking on our lawn,
   Inscribed in rainbow letters on the queenly brow of dawn,
We read the words, they thrill our blood beneath our coat of tan,
   "You're camping on the clover trails of Smiling Michigan".

Stewart Douglas
June 9, 1931

SOURCES OF STRENGTH

Strength comes to him who deems a thing worth trying,
And gives himself to do it with a will –
His weakness by his action thus denying,
And giving stronger men a wholesome thrill.

Strength comes to him who keeps a happy courage,
And lays the odds that he shall win his task,
And gambles that he'll never pay demurrage –
And will not stoop an even chance to ask.

Strength comes to him, tho weak and frail his body,
Whose spirit kindles to a steady flame,
Eschewing all that's mean and low and shoddy,
Whose life is guided by a noble aim.

Strength comes to him – 'tis now a common story –
Who marks himself the last for any gift.
He wraps himself around with deathless glory,
Who helps the world its heavy burden lift.

Stewart Douglas

THE SPARROW

Wherever you go they are sure to be there,
The commonest bird that flies in the air,
And because they are common and with us all year
If they fell by the thousand we'd not shed a tear.
They are targets for boys and they're targets for men,
And the automobile runs them down now and then.
We feel since they're here we've a license to harrow
And hold in contempt the plain life of the sparrow.

Can nothing be said for this bird that's so common?
This bird with the everyday, simple cognomen,
This bird that is with us when summer is dying –
Aye, with us tho climate be freezing or frying,
This bird you find perched on the bare leafless branch,
Or out on the prow of your wave-cutting launch.
This bird that precedes e'en the actions of men,
Far southward and northward, - surpassing our ken.

Deep in the hearts and the annals of men
Is recorded a place for the Linty and Wren,
But praise – who would give to a bird like the Sparrow?
Whose living by this is restricted and narrow.
But tho our regard for this plain feathered bird
Is less than a cipher in action and word
When the others have flown with the speed of the arrow
Thru snow, sleet and rain – bides the "stay with it" sparrow.

Yes, merit there is in this bird that's so plain
The merit to suffer contumely and pain,
The merit to hardily breast every breeze
Where summer suns shine or running brooks freeze.
Unsung, unrenowned, little bird of the air
Of burdens we know you have more than your share
Yet tho cheery your life or distressing your fall,
You were noted by Him who looks after us all.

Stewart Douglas

STARS LOOK DOWN

The stars look down from their vaulted heights
On the fitful scenes below
On the usual sights of the lighted nights
Where men pass to and fro
Where the tearless eye and the haughty mien
Wots not of the woe or pain
That others glean tho' their souls are clean
After sowing the golden grain.

The stars look down, do they look in vain?
Or are they but soulless orbs?
Could their knowledge pass to these hearts of brass?
There might be responsive chords
And the undimmed eye and the barren pride
Of the slumbering son's of men
Like mists of the night would vanish from sight
And never return again.

But the stars look down and continue to stare
As they've stared for weary years
On the pain and joy of the man and boy
And the stars have shed their tears
And the selfish years of the world roll on
And countless lives are shriven
For the harshness of men is the world's greatest bane
And the greatest surprise to Heaven.

Stewart Douglas

STRIPES

Stripes, stripes, day and night stripes
Burned in the brain of me
Part of the grain of me
Ever the shame of me
Tarnishing, unmoral stripes.

Stripes, stripes, unmanning stripes
Writ on the heart of me
Parcel and part of me
Daggers they dart at me
Murdering, murdering stripes.

Stripes, stripes red branding stripes
They're with me for ever
Escape from them never
For none may deliver
From soul searing, immortal stripes.

Stripes, stripes, circular stripes
The forger must wear them
The robber must bare them
The innocent share them
There is no division in stripes.

Stripes, stripes, pitiful stripes
They'll doggedly follow you
Branding they'll call to you
Finally swallow you
Merciless, merciless stripes.

Stewart Douglas

A STROLL IN THE RAIN

There's a love in my heart for the pattering rain,
As it falls thru the day or the night,
A love in my heart that I cannot explain
That everywhere sets the world right.
All the world's looking fine when the rains gently fall
With their soothing effect on my brain,
And with rubbers and coat I can hear the glad call,
O come on for a stroll in the rain.

There's a love in my heart for the battering rain,
As it batters my window and door,
A love in my heart that repeats the refrain
Of a wind–driven rain on a moor.
All the poetry and music that wells in my heart,
The romance of the old country lane,
Inexpressible are from the moment I start
For a stroll in the wind–driven rain.

There's a love in my heart for the musical rain
As it beats on the old window sill,
A love that responds to the soft, mellow strain
Falling gently on meadow and rill.
There's a trill and a thrill in my heart when it pours
Or when lightly it pats on the pane
But the joy of it all is for me out–of–doors
When I stroll in the God–given rain.

Stewart Douglas

THE SUCCESS OF SUCCESS

It may shine in the gleam of a smile,
It may lurk in the long second mile;
It is there in the beauty of Mother,
It may lie in the tear for another.
Men may see it, but you may not know it,
None may see it, and still your life show it.
This thing called success in the showing
Lies not in the reaping but sowing.

It may lie in a pathway that's drear,
Or come through the conquering of fear;
It may rest in a shadow or token, -
Will you know it when loud it has spoken?
You may reach it and think it escapes you,
It's the reaching that molds you and makes you.
Success is not merely arriving,
The good of success is the striving.

Stewart Douglas

A THANKSGIVING HOPE

As man to man and friend to friend
I'm thinking of you here,
Of joy, of hope, the charm of life,
And all that you revere;
And thinking in the firelight glow
This thought comes straight and true,
I'm hoping that God will sup
Always with yours and you.

Stewart Douglas

THAT'S A DIFFERENT STORY

Smile when the tempest is raging,
Smile tho' your heart be as lead.
Smile, is the message you give me,
Tho' around me are scattered the dead.
But what if the wild winds retreating,
Meet you with the same awful force.
That's a different story, my brother,
A different story, of course.

Be strong, when the fortress is crumbling,
Be strong, when your citadel falls.
In the heart of the message you give me,
Tho' you're deaf when an hour of need calls.
But what, when your own castle trembles,
When battered by just the same force,
That's a different story, my brother,
A different story, of course.

Be merciful, kindly, and tender,
Be loving as He was of old.
In the message of comfort you bring me,
Tho' my children are suffering from cold.
But what if the same ruthless fortune,
Should bring to your child even worse.
That's a different story, my brother,
A different story, of course.

Give, tho' your fortune be slender,
Give, and I'm willing, God knows,
In the heart of the message you bring me,
To relieve the world's sorrow and woes.
But what when the world's needy millions,
Bids you to unloosen your purse.
That's a different story, my brother,
A different story, of course.

Stewart Douglas
January 17, 1935

THE TASK OF A MAN

To arise from the grave of a past wholly dark
And to face the world bravely alone,
In the power of a purpose ennobled by love
For the sins of the past to atone.

To go forward unerringly, patiently true
The soul growing bigger each day
To grasp the importance of things that are real
To be always prepared for the fray.

To unselfishly give when it means only loss,
And in sympathy spreading good cheer
And when others less capable lead in the van
Content to be found in the rear.

To sow in the knowledge that others will reap,
Doing always the best that one can,
Holding steady to truth and the purpose of love
Is the task and the test of a man.

Stewart Douglas

THEIR STANDARD

They shoot out their lip and they stare with their eyes,
Insolent eyes, eyes that despise,
And they tell without trying to all who are wise,
To the near and the far just what they are.
Yet tho they are known there's a hurt in their stare
That makes a man feel, that makes a man reel,
They speak with their eye what their lips wouldn't dare,
That a poor man would steal 'cause he's down at the heel.

Their arrogant pose and their whispering skill,
Whispers that spread, whispers of dread,
Thru the sensitive soul sends their life-sapping chill
Till the tottering strength almost measures its length.
Thus arrogance, pride, with their soul-searing tools
On a luckless man frowns, on his ups and his downs,
And so speaking plain, he'll be breaking the rules,
For he's down at the heel and of course he would steal.

So edging your way through the long crowded lanes
Of a life that's replete with hope and defeat,
Remember that after the clouds and the rains
There's an ear to the wheat that will taste the more sweet.
Tho suspicion may mark you and wound you withal
There's a thrill to all life, there's a thrill to all strife,
And tho down at the heel just keep chasing the ball,
With your eye on the goal and a strong honest soul.

Stewart Douglas

THERE'S SOMETHING TO BE DONE

When lying in port you must see to the anchor,
When sailing the seas you must see to your sail,
When "Lizzie" is stalled why of course you must crank her,
By now you believe this is merely a tale.
Yet whether you're resting or whether you're playing,
Or working and toiling with vigor and zest,
There's something to see to, it goes without saying
If you would keep fit and in trim for the best.

There's always a task just beyond what you're doing,
Beyond the day's rest or the glamour and strife,
But out of each task to your soul comes accruing
The strength and the sum and the substance of life.
So whether you're planning a week end vacation,
A joyous old time with a number of friends,
Or planning your work with a mental elation
There'll always be something to do till it ends.

Stewart Douglas

THOUGHTS IN A CHURCHYARD

Sleeping so quietly, your slumber unbroken,
Starlight and daylight mean nothing to you,
Aeons and ages but myths that are spoken,
Only the living may know they are true,
Free from the cares that the living must gather,
Here where the tears of the world soak the ground,
Here where a mother or sister or father
Or some other loved one is marked by a mound.

Eerie the winds that are now blowing o'er you,
Lonesome the feeling from each covered bier,
But what are the feelings of those who adore you
Remembering with anguish the day you came here, -
Here where the pain of true hearts will not banish,
Here where the tears of the living must flow,
Here where the presence of loved ones must vanish,
Here where we conquer our bitterest foe.

Stewart Douglas

THOUGHTS IN THE OPEN

A silent world, a dreamful world,
A sleeping world but me,
Save for the sounds that come from night
And nature's melody.
Singing a song to the soul o' me,
Ravishing every thought,
Where a star-spangled Heaven roofs in my house,
And the green grass makes my cot.

This is a world where a shrine is laid
To all that's fine and white,
Where the darkest thought may be transformed
Till formed of the whitest light.
Where voices formed of the silent deep
Their coded message sends,
And the look I see in a million eyes
Is the look of a million friends.

So give me this world where the dust is still
And the cleansing silence reigns,
Where the night broadcasts to the heart attuned
A thousand mellowing strains, --
Or set me down when the night is past
And the morning sun has ris'n,
Where the laughing, gurgling streams run by,
And my soul will leap to Heaven.

Stewart Douglas

THOUGHTS ON EASTER

Dark is the night and drab the day
With leaden skies for June and May;
A starless world where'er you turn
Where man was only "made to mourn",
Where future aeons give no hope
And death's supreme and God's remote.

Fair spring may come and blossom forth
And fragrant winds blow east and north
But mouldering dust to dust must lie
Beneath an austere frowning sky –
And soul and spirit, what were they?
Had God withheld an Easter day.

But budding spring and bursting flow'r
Now sets the day, bespeaks the hour
When Death itself forever dies,
When all shall in full dress arise
And mingle in the grand display
That consummates our Easter day.

Stewart Douglas

TOAST OF THE FATHERS TO THE SONS

To the Lads who'll follow after,
To the Lads of merry Laughter,
To the Lads of many graces,
To the Lads who'll take our places, -
Tis for you this toast is given, -
Lads for whom we've fought and striven, -
May each Lad where lads foregather
Raise the standard of his Father.

Stewart Douglas

TO A YOUNG MOTHER

The skies will now seem softer to you, dear,
Life's meaning richer, deeper, full and clear;
And tho' you've paid the price all mothers pay,
Full glory touches all your life today,
And on your brow the gift that God call's "good",
The crowning beauty of your motherhood.

How deep the joy that now must fill your breast;
The poets say it cannot be express'd.
The angels tried to sing this joy of old,
But you must know how much they left untold,
When unto you – O joy – a son was giv'n,
And God's rare smile came down to you from Heav'n.

Stewart Douglas

TOGETHER

You need me and I need you
How much we need each other
The whole wide world is kith and kin
And every man's our brother.
The things we need are the needs of all
And the things we do our measure
Selfless love is the highest gain
And the surest road to pleasure.

You need me and I need you
'Tis an ancient, ancient story
The world will bleed in the ebb and tide
Of its struggle up to glory
Your strength's a myth when you lift alone
And mine, - the weight of a feather
The world will rise, but it never can
'Til both of us lift together.

Stewart Douglas

THE TRAIL OF THE KING

I watched him go by; I was here for a rest,
In that little quiet place in the land of the west
And my heart gave a bound, --here's a man among men
My decision to follow I made there and then.
This lion–like man with the falcon eye clear
I would find what his mission was here in St. Vere.
So he led and I followed, yes right in his track
But he held on his way nor even glanced back.
Straight to the heart of his mission he went
Like a true man of purpose, or one Heaven sent,
He opened the door of a house in the vale
Where poverty reigned, where the parents were frail,
I waited for hours till the stranger came forth
I wanted to know what his actions were worth.
But the look on his face showed without an alloy
He had drunk from the spring of the world's purest joy
He'd been blessing humanity-- doing his best
While being at ease in this land of the west.
So the draperies rolled from the years of the past
And my selfishness stood clear before me at last.
To taste such a joy as this stranger had known
Would be Heaven for anyone here or at home.
And from that day to this I have sampled such joy
As I never had known as a man or a boy.
And the stranger I tracked in that land of the west
I have found in his footsteps the calm of deep rest.
And with reverence I've wondered and reasoned by law
It must have been Jesus, the King that I saw.

Stewart Douglas

TRANSCENDENT AMERICA

Free as the untrammeled, unfettered eagle
Strong as the tides of the wind-drivin seas,
Tried as the oak that has stood the gale's lashing,
Tenderly sung by the voice of the breeze.
Calm as the haze of a mid-summer's morning,
Full of rich mercy, but hating the wrong,
O how it reaches the depths of our being –
Land of the stars and the stripes and our song.

CHORUS
Then come let us sing for our colors are flying,
The Pride of America waves in the sun.
Land of the stars and the stripes and our glory,
God keep us true to the freedom we won.

Grand as the beauty that lives in the sunset,
True as the colors that blend in her flag,
Mountain and valley her praises resounding,
Prowess acclaimed from the peak of each crag,
Rev'rence and love in the heart of her people,
The stars of her banner burnished to gold, --
God writes her story, immortal her glory, --
Land of the fearless, the peerless, the bold.

CHORUS
Then come let us sing for our colors are flying,
The Pride of America waves in the sun.
Land of the stars and the stripes and our glory,
God keep us true to the freedom we won.

Stewart Douglas
August 6, 1928

TRUE DESIRE

How eagerly the little hands
Will do a mother's will
The little feet, how swift her errands run,
And gladness fills the heart of ev'ry little boy or girl
When night finds something for a mother done.
And eagerly their little minds will scan the distant time
To where in earnest they'll be maids or men
And in the distant future you may see enshrined a queen
Ah – for mother they will make it easy then.

How gladly will a little girl
Go trilling to the task
Of cleaning up when Mother's going slow
And sometimes with the wisdom that is far beyond her years
She'll whisper, "Daddy, take Ma to a show."
And gladly too a little boy will dig in with a grin
Just to give a boy's best friend a needed rest.
But boy and girl alike love best the vision of the day
When they can give to Ma the very best.

How happy too, a mother's look
When watching her dear boy
A-chopping wood or laughing in his play
And how she smiles when Mary says, "I'll wash the dishes, Ma."
I'd love to work for mumsy all the day
And so the heart of children is the heart of true desire,
The best for mother when they're maids or men
But children work with all your strength and pray with all your soul
That in you she'll not be disappointed then.

Stewart Douglas
1922

TRYING SITUATIONS

I can list to a garrulous woman,
For her I may stifle the yawn,
Tho she carry my mind to the moment
When perpetual motion may dawn.
I can bear the quick play of her features
As her words show the change of her moods,
But I'd run like a deer from the garrulous man
And lose myself deep in the woods.

I can even find joy in the moonlight,
Tho a garrulous woman be near,
I am safe when it's dark if she's with me,
For she sounds like a regiment I fear.
But the hardest of all situations,
And the one I'll escape if I can,
Is to find when I'm hungry and dining,
Right beside me, a garrulous man.

Stewart Douglas

TWO ROSES

Two lovely roses side by side
By a narrow pathway grew,
Smiling up at the rising sun,
Sipping the morning dew.

One lean'd back from the trodden path,
Modest and fair to behold, -
One lean'd close to the passers-by,
Fragrant, but over-bold.

Two fair young lives by a warm hearth
Grew up in a love–warm air,
Shelter'd from ev'ry ill or harm,
Kept from the dregs of care.

One inclin'd to the tempting throng,
A beautiful sparkling youth, -
One in modesty kept her faith
And heart with fireside truth.

Two roses red in a morn'in fair
Grew each from an ample root, -
The sun rose high, one lay crush'd and
Bruis'd by a wanton foot.

Stewart Douglas

UNPAID

Over the dying and bones of the dead
A great many vows have been made
Vows that had better been left all unsaid
For the greater part's never been paid.
Only the soothing of conscience were they
For the nonce maybe earnest and true
Then gone like the mists at the herald of day
Or sapped like the morn's early dew.

Over the graves of our own better selves
We've made many and many a vow
That we'd rise from the ashes and put on the shelves
The things we're indulging in now
But jestingly telling us, grim tho the jest
That weak are the vows we have made.
We know we shall never in life reach the best
Till all of our vows have been paid.

Stewart Douglas

VALUES

There are some things in life can be measured,
Yes, sometimes the things of the heart,
Tho' these may be valued and treasured,
Of you be an integral part.
Yet others no measure or plummet
Has yet been designed that can reach
To the depths or the height or the summit
Of the value of all or of each.

And tho' love has a service eternal,
And to life adds its most priceless gifts,
There's a faith and a joy that's supernal,
And it beckons, it stoops and it lifts,
It's the spirit of sympathy laving,
It's the touch of another's fine soul,
The encouraging look that is saving, -
And thrusting you on to your goal.

Stewart Douglas

THE VANITY OF WORDS

"Old friend, don't be down-hearted,
For see the clouds have parted,
And behold, the sun is shining on your door."
"O yes, the sun's adorning
This gleaming, mocking morning,
But, -The waves have cast my dead upon the shore."

"Look up, the flood's subsiding,
Faith, home and love abiding, -
Beauty springs from even the smallest bud."
"O yes, there's even beauty
Within a sense of duty, -
But who'll return my lost ones from the flood."

"Look, friend, the day's advancing
All living things are dancing, -
The flow'rs are blooming, see the rose is red." –
"O yes, your words so glowing,
May help my children knowing,
Their father's out of work and out of bread."

"Old friend, my tears are falling,
God help these days, - appalling, -
My feeble words your woes can nev'r mend."
"O yes, your tears are better
Than words by mouth or letter,
For words but mock the anguish of a friend."

Stewart Douglas

WELCOME

Hail! Welcome tae oor bonnie toon,
And should you chance tae look aroon
We hope you'll see in us a boon,
Aye, tae the very letter.
Yet for a while we'll sadly note
That this wee toon has "got your goat"
And often we may hear you quote,
"The auld, auld toon is better".

Yet frien'ly hearts are ayn the same,
Across the border or at hame
And frien'ship is this wee toon's aim,
That's why we pu' t'gether.
But when the auld scenes cry aloud
Believe us you'll be understood
You'll find us fitting every mood
And true as Scottish heather.

So doubly welcome tae this toon
And when you flash your een aroon
May a' the lights that shine abune
Reveal your way say clearly,
That as you live from day to day
You'll feel Bay City's blithe and gay
And some day we will hear you say
Auld toon I loe you dearly.

Stewart Douglas

WHAT A SMILE MAY DO

I never thought that a smile on your face
Could do for me what it's done,
Where darkness reigned in my hopeless soul
I now catch a glimpse of the sun.
From a wanderer over the face of the globe
To contentment beside my own hearth
Your smile like the Day has retouched the cold clay
And a dead soul's been given rebirth.

I never thought that a smile could thus show
The warmth of a heart beneath.
And I'd give of my all if I to my race
Could such a blessing bequeath.
For there's nothing that gauges the worth of a man
Like a smile – 'tis the torch of the soul
That welcomes and cheers while it banishes fears
Or a wandering cynic makes whole.

Stewart Douglas

WHAT MORTALS WE

Man has fought for every creed
Supporting each with reddened deed,
And bartered body, soul and Heav'n
For things he thought the Lord had giv'n.

Through weary wars he's glanced above
And prayed for mercy, peace, and love,
Then plunged with conscience all a–smother
To spear a weary hearted brother.

When all the world's serene and fair
He sits uneasy in his chair, -
The peace of God he would despoil,
This lover of the world's turmoil.

Stewart Douglas

WHAT OF YOU

In the far off frozen regions,
In the wild and trackless north
Where the foot of man has seldom ever trod,
Where your reason stumbles, falters,
Where you see a thousand altars
Dedicated to the presence of a God.

On the sunny slopes when morning
Spreads its glory on the sea,
And you calmly view this marvel deep and broad,
There your wonder but increases
While your logic goes to pieces,
As the waters tell the story of a God.

In the silent evening's glory
When the lights are lit above
And the trees are casting shadows on the sod,
Subtle thoughts that come to tease you
Will depart and there will seize you
A sense of the approaching steps of God.

In the mansion or the hovel
Where the lights burn high or low,
Where life seems gilt with splendor, or a fraud,
With prejudice behind you
And a clear head to remind you
Behind the scenes you'll see the print of God.

Since the frozen lands and sunny
And the morning on the sea,
And the gleaming night and stars their Maker laud,
As you journey o'er life's highway
On the open road or byway
You'll discover the sublimity of God

Stewart Douglas

WHEN MA'S AWAY

We know not what's come over Pa since Mama went away
For rest and quiet beside the healthful sea,
But every day he seems unlike the Paw we used to know
When Ma prepared his supper and his tea.
Sometimes he'll try to laugh and dance around with all us kids
But then the humor quickly passes off,
And then that blamed old grouch will take a hold of him inside
And at everything he'll start to rave and scoff.

He never used to carry on like this when Maw was 'round,
He was always just as pleasant as could be
And still at times he tries to work the old mood up again
And then we're glad to dance around his knee.
But oh! It doesn't last at all, just like a dream at night
That passes with the rising O' the sun,
And then he's finding fault with all we try to do or say
And that leaves all us children very glum.

But yet we love our Pa for tho he's cross he's never mean
And he's just been cross since Mama had to leave
And we know 'twould make a difference if Mama just came home
For when she left how Papa sure did grieve.
Ah! Ma's do make a difference to Pa's when they're around
And the gloom goes out when Mama brings her light
And when Ma comes home we'll hug her tight and love her oh! so much
And we know that Ma will set our Papa right.

Stewart Douglas

WOMAN

Regal but tender
Changeful but true
Buoyant but steady,
Fresh as the dew.
Sparkling today,
Placid tomorrow,
Soothing the world,
Nursing its sorrow.

Prideful but gentle
Sadful but sweet
Laurels of nations
Lie at her feet.
Simple yet wise,
Mellow as May,
Senates and Kingdoms
Under her sway.

Frail in her strength
Yet stronger than we
Sceptered by Heav'n
And worshipped by me.
Mistress of home
And of destinies too,
Exalted the nation
That gives her her due.

Of such are our sweethearts
Of such are our wives,
Of such are the mothers
Who plan out our lives.
Wrap round me forever
The arms of these three,
Purity, Goodness,
Love deep as the sea.

Stewart Douglas

THE WONDERFUL JEW

Israel beloved of God since Abraham was called,
Down the teeming years you've come, footsore but unappalled.

Footsore through journeys hard and wild, through winding ways and long,
You've kept faiths steady flame alight, through tears, and aches and song.

The ages marvel at your strength, a nation without voice,
A nation scattered o'er the Earth and left without a choice.

And wonder fills the mind of man – you've trodden straight nor swerved,
And wonder puts the question thus, how have you been preserv'd?

Through years of bitter strife and blood, through agonies so keen,
How have you kept your race intact, inviolate, serene?

"Go search the books of yesterday," your answer thus is giv'n, -
"Go search where hearts and minds were pierc'd and human souls were riv'n"

"Go search where red seas stood before and Phar'ohs pressed behind,
Where Earth and Hell their forces met to crush a nation's mind"

"Go search the barren hills of Earth, the desert's blasting suns,
Go seek the dying and the lost where ev'ry river runs"

"Go search the valleys and the plains, where bleach a million bones,
Where still the winds of Heav'n are thick, with little children's moans"

"Go search the fearful spite of men, its blasting, scourging rod,
The answer why we're still preserv'd you'll find alone – is God."

The world and all therein must stand aghast if this be true,
If God has kept inviolate the persecuted Jew.

And here's where mystery deepens, and here's where questions rise,
Why should the world condemn or scorn or look with hating eyes?

On such a people, such a race, who brought the nation its rest,
Who gave the world far greater men, than any nation's best.

Who gave the world its living Lord, its creed, - the highest pric'd, -
Who brought the light to gentile hearts, who gave the world its Christ;

Who gave the world its finest book, who wielded such a pen,
Who wrote religion in the rocks and in the hearts of men;

Who gave the world its Marys pure, the tender gentle kind,
Whose pow'r is felt in mart and home to soothe the wounded mind.

But what have they in giving thus, save only world-wide spleen,
And hissing words and scathing looks by village, town or green.

In groups they're curs'd by lesser men, in ones and threes and twos,
Condemn'd by nations far beneath the mighty handed Jews.

With spite and malice criticized, because – though not by chance –
Their keen-eyed minds have made them kings in realms of world finance.

Yet battleships – they have not one, navies, armies, neither,
Nor planes that carry death conceal'd swimming through the ether.

The snorting horse but loses breath, like men who beat the air,
'Twere better far to save one's strength and treat the issue fair;

To see that unto ev'ry race is giv'n a horse to ride
Though Israel's horse be golden-hued, why should she be denied?

But reason? That has long since fled when dealing with a race
Who put to death so long ago the Lord of light and grace.

Their evil deed remembered well and crimes that they have done,
The good? How easily forgot though blazoned in the sun.

Then sages of the wide world o'er this question's asked of you,
If you had filled the place and stead of ev'ry ancient Jew,

What would your judgment there have been, how wise your thought and word,
Would you have known that face serene, would you have known the Lord?

Then pass not judgment on a race who did what you would do,
Did e'en the Lord appear again to other than the Jew.

But scan their problem deep and real, their grasp and mode of life,
And honor give where honor's due, instead of blood and strife.

Then only as your thoughts turn back across the sands of time,
Shall dawn the pregnant meaning, full of faith that is sublime.

Of faith that saves through thick and thin, wherever man has trod,
And proves the sons of Jacob are the strongest proof of God.

Stewart Douglas

WONDERS

Fresh wonders all along our way comes tripping with each dawn
The golden shades of morning and the flowers with dew thereon,
The glories of the future and the conquests of the past
The mighty thoughts of mighty men in molds of glory cast;
New beauties from the soul of art by laymen and by Deans
From lips of inspiration and the flowing pen of Queens –
But AH! The breathless wonders that have left mind and heart askance,
When walking down the starry lanes and landscapes of Romance.

New stars appear, new twilights come, new pictures in the fire,
New wonders in a loving eye whereof we never tire;
New notes discovered or disclosed when listening to the birds
The happy laugh of childhood whose enjoyment naught disturbs –
But who shall tell the wonders as we tripped the Milky Way,
In and out among the stars, - O glistening nights and gay!
Or speak the thoughts that filled us with the spirit of the dance,
When walking through the glades and glens and landscapes of Romance.

Stewart Douglas

THE WORST KIND

This world is composed of a great many folks
From the clown to the prince and the maker of jokes
And the folks that we meet in the course of our time
Have as many queer moods as a maker of rhyme.
There are some who are restless like waters that roll,
And some who are calloused in spirit and soul.
There are some who are cranky – but hear old Bill Hutchie
"The Lord steer me clear of the folks who are touchy".

There are folks who conspire to lead you a dance –
Their fond disposition you know in advance,
There are others who threaten and bluster through life,
And where'ver you go you'll find breeders of strife.
There are world–famous people who're never content
Unless they are raising your ire or your rent.
And folks who are fussy – Hear old William Hutchie,
"The Lord steer me clear of the folks who are touchy".

There are folks who are sour – you must know the class.
And folks with a nature as brazen as brass,
There are some who can laugh when the tear drop should fall
And some who for others will give up their all.
There are folks who are funny and witty and wise
And folks who are living in perfect disguise,
But again let me utter the prayer of old Hutchie,
"The Lord steer me clear of the folks who are touchy".

Stewart Douglas

A YOUNG LAUGH

Dedicated to Mrs. Grant Moors.
Inspired by Douglas Moors when he was a boy about two.

O it's just the laugh of a boy of two,
But Oh! How it thrills you thru and thru, –
And couldn't you run for a couple of miles
On the strength of one of his winsome smiles.

What witchery lies in his gurgling Laugh,
When his eyes light up you feel that the chaff
Of your life for the nonce has been blown away,
And you stand in the light of a purer day.

Who wouldn't face life with a happier grin
Who wouldn't respond when he dimples his chin
Who wouldn't be kinder, more honest and true,
When wrapped in the smile of a boy about two.

Stewart Douglas

Epilogue

STRANGE DREAM
January 11, 1945

I was walking down the street of an ancient town, tall majestic buildings on each side. I don't know the name of the town or country. Suddenly I found myself abreast of a company of American soldiers. Then a tall, strong-faced young fellow broke from the ranks and cried, "Heavenly music, it's grandpa!" Then he nearly squeezed the breath out of me and said, "Cling to the old faith grandpa, it's the only thing worth clinging to." Then he dashed back, saying "I've broken the rules now. I'll be seeing you." I looked at the commander, for the company had stopped, and I said, "Don't hold it against him, sir." And he answered, "I won't, Reverend sir." Then I awoke.

Stewart Douglas

*Note: On Novemeber 14, 1945, his oldest grandson was killed in France while serving in the Army Air Corps. (WSM)

Postlude

Since William has told you about Stewart, let me tell you about William. A richly deserved patriarch in his own right, he lived the moral responsibility towards his church and community. While supporting the arts, music, education, and in his full time job as President of the Alpena Alcona Area Governmental Employees Credit Union, William Stewart Moors was a servant to his fellow human.

He created magnificent wood carvings and had a love for the local sea – Lake Huron. He served his country in the Korean War and was a great friend to the Boy Scouts of America. He once built an old fashioned automobile, the Gazelle, from pieces. When it was finished, we rode it in the Alpena 4th of July parade and I threw candy to all the kids.

An avid piper, William studied with the great Sandy Jones in the mountains of North Carolina on bagpipes purchased from a little shop in Edinburgh, Scotland. He played frequently at events in the town. Sometimes he would haunt the beach at sunset.

William loved his family of three sons, wife, and grandchildren. He was also a great lover of pets, always having a dog by his side. For years it was Springer spaniels, and in his later years the Scottish terrier aptly named Mackey.

William S. Moors was a member of the School Board, and a Lay Minister at his church. He built the very cross in the centerpiece of the building that he headed the committee to build. He was also instrumental in creating the Alpena band shell where countless people now enjoy music.

After a long day at work, William could be found reclining with a pipe and spinning a yarn. Warm and fellowship minded, 'Bill' as many friends knew him, was a giant, wholly fulfilling the spirit imbued in him by Stewart Douglas.

It is amazing that this book is dedicated to grandfathers, as I, the eldest grandson of William S. Moors, who was the grandson of Stewart Douglas, take up with duty and honor the publication of this work.

It is my dearest hope that it will strengthen my own family and enrich any who would care to share.

Blessings and still keeping the faith,

Christopher M. Moors, 2012

www.ingramcontent.com/pod-product-compliance
Lightning Source LLC
Chambersburg PA
CBHW080338170426
43194CB00014B/2609